The Complete SEO 2014 & Beyond

SEO 2014 & Beyond + SEO Checklist Bundle

By Dr. Andy Williams

http://ezseonews.com

Version 2.0

22nd January 2014

The Complete SEO 2014 & Beyond

Includes: SEO 2014 & Beyond + SEO Checklist Bundle

This book contains my 2 popular SEO books in a single volume:

SEO 2014 & Beyond

Search Engine Optimization will never be the same again

Google Panda seems to penalize low quality content, whereas Penguin is more concerned about overly aggressive SEO tactics. Stuff that SEOs had been doing for years, not only doesn't work anymore, but now can cause your site to be penalized and drop out of the rankings. Just about everything you have been taught about SEO in the last 10 years can be thrown out the Window. Google have moved the goal posts. In this book, I want to share with you the new SEO, the SEO for 2014 and Beyond.

SEO Checklist

A step-by-step plan for fixing SEO problems with your web site.

It provides a step-by-step plan to fix a broken site and contains detailed checklists with an explanation of why those things are important. These checklists are based on the SEO that I use on a daily basis. It's the SEO I teach my students, and it's the SEO that I know works. For those that embrace the recent changes, SEO has actually become easier as we no longer have to battle against other sites whose SEO was done 24/7 by an automated tool or an army of cheap labor. Those sites have largely been removed, and that levels the playing field. If you have a site that lost rankings, this book gives you a step-by-step action plan and checklist to fix problems that are common causes of ranking penalties.

The Complete SEO 2014 & Beyond

BOOK 1 – SEO 2014 & BEYOND

Book 2 - An SEO Checklist

DISCLAIMER AND TERMS OF USE AGREEMENT

SEO

2014 And Beyond

Search engine optimization will never be the same again!

By Dr. Andy Williams

ezSEONews

Creating Fat Content

Version 2.0.

Released: 6th December 2013

What people said about "SEO 2013 & Beyond"

"Read this book and anything else you can get your hands on by this guy."

"Dr. Andy Williams is to my mind the man to listen to when it comes to the subject of building a website in a clean ethical manner. His explanations of what Google and the other search engines consider as part of the ranking process cannot be bettered. If you wish to create a long lived website that does not need to fear the latest Google update(s) then pay heed." **Jim**

"After 10 years online building and promoting websites, I became quite adept at SEO (both on-page and off), but that was then, and this is now! Having read this eBook from cover to cover, I think you would be hard pressed to find more informative, descriptive, and easy-to-understand material on the subject of present day SEO anywhere." **Andy Aitch**

"This is the right way to build websites. There is a slot of rubbish written by many so-called experts, but this is not one of them. If you want to learn the best way to do SEO, then this is the leading book I have read, and I have read many." **Dobsy "Dobsy" (UK)**

"Basically I loved this book and highly recommend it. It is the best couple bucks you will ever spend. It is easy to read, succinct, and brilliant. He offers a lot of great tips without all the fluff that some authors throw in to add page count. Thanks Andy for a good read that upped my SEO IQ." **Nicole Bernd**

"Since Penguin was released in April 2012, SEO has been turned on its head. Creating themed content with LSI in mind, instead of keyword focused content, is now the way to go.

Amazingly, this is exactly what Andy has been teaching for the past ten years. I only wished I had known him when I started out in internet marketing as his style of teaching is the best. He's a very genuine and generous person and if you've been hit by Panda or Penguin, this book is exactly what you need." **Carole**

"Great book, super helpful and makes seo easy to understand, especially for ecommerce novice! Would definitely recommend to anyone trying to get a handle on best practices in seo." **cswaff**

"He was warning of a Panda type hit at least two years before the Panda was born. Although the Penguin has changed things more than a bit, in this book, Dr Andy clearly, and in simple terminology, explains the strategies and tactics needed to stay on the good side of Google." **Tony Crofts**

"Great at teaching the difference in old SEO practices vs. New techniques." **Ms. WriterGirl**

"Andy is one of the few people that I listen to when it comes to SEO because rather than "follow the usual crowd", that tends to share rehashed information with little value that's based on fact, he does his own testing to determine what is actually working for him, and then shares his own results." **J. Stewart**

"This book was a very quick and easy read from start to finish. I found it to be an excellent work with some very mature insight into the nuances of how to get in good graces with Google. It took a few of my beliefs and approaches to Search Engine Optimization and turned them upside down." **Jonathan W. Walker**

"This is ground breaking Internet marketing information. Stuff you won't find elsewhere. Being a longtime pupil of Dr. Andy, I have put much of it to the test myself and I know it proves out. If you are in the Internet business, you need to read this book." **Norman Morrison**

"After following Andy Williams for over 8 years now I had a hunch his new SEO, 2013 & Beyond would be a winner . . . and it is. Simple, straight forward and on target with respect to the latest updates, upgrades, and algorithmic mods by our friends at Google. Do what Andy teaches, especially with reference to great content creation, and you will be successful in your SEO efforts." **Chris Cobb**

DISCLAIMER AND TERMS OF USE AGREEMENT

Pre & post Penguin SEO

On February 11th, 2011, Google released the Panda update. The update was designed to filter out low quality web pages from the index. This was necessary because an earlier release (codenamed caffeine) massively increased the number of web pages that Google needed to handle - much of which was low quality. At the time, Panda left webmasters scratching their heads as to why their sites were penalized. The answer was simple – their pages were not deemed sufficient quality.

On 24th April 2012, Google unleashed the Penguin. If Panda was a 1 on the Richter scale of updates, Penguin was surely a 10. It completely changed the way we needed to think about SEO. It seems that Penguin's job was to find web pages that had been optimized beyond the "tolerance level" for that site, and punish them accordingly. That's right, just about everything you have been taught about SEO in the last 10 years can be thrown out the Window. Google has moved the goal posts.

On 22nd May 2013, Google unleashed Penguin 2.0 which went far deeper than the original Penguin algorithm. This was not just a data refresh, but a major update to Penguin itself, and it's only going to get tougher.

On 26th September 2013 Google announced yet another update, called Hummingbird. This update had actually rolled out around the 20th August 2013, but this one is less likely to have caused you problems than Panda or Penguin. We'll look at Hummingbird a little later.

Fast-forward to today…

Ask a bunch of webmasters to define the term SEO and I bet you'll get a lot of different answers. I'm sure that three of the most common phrases you'll hear are on-page factors, off-page factors, and link building.

Definitions of SEO will differ depending on the type of person you ask and even when you ask them. SEO before Google introduced the Panda update was easy. After the Panda update it was still relatively easy, but you needed to make sure your content was good. After Google released the Penguin update, SEO suddenly became a whole lot harder. Let me explain this with a diagram:

SEO Pre-Panda & Penguin

← Increasingly Safe   Increasingly Risky →

White Hat SEO

Black Hat SEO

Strategies Google tolerate

Strategies Google DO NOT tolerate

In the diagram above, I have noted two forms of SEO:

1. **White Hat SEO** – approved strategies for getting your page to rank well. Google offers guidelines to webmasters which spell out approved SEO strategies (search Google for Webmaster guidelines).
2. **Black Hat SEO** – strategies that Google dislike and would like to penalize. These include a whole host of strategies from on-page keyword stuffing to backlinking blasts using software to generate tens of thousands of backlinks to your site.

If you think of this as a sliding scale from totally safe "White Hat" SEO to totally dangerous "Black Hat" SEO, then you can imagine that as you move to the right with your SEO, you are more likely to get into hot water with Google (at least in the long term). As you move more to the left with your SEO, you are more likely to be safer with Google.

Before Panda & Penguin, most webmasters knew where the lines were drawn and took their risks accordingly.

When Google introduced Panda, the only real change to this was that webmasters now needed to make sure that the content on their website was unique, interesting to visitors, AND added something that maybe no other webpage on the topic had. No small task, but to beat Panda, which is essentially a Google add-on that looks for quality, this is our target.

When Google introduced Penguin, they completely changed the face of SEO, probably forever, or at least as long as Google continues to be the dominant search engine. Here is a diagrammatic representation of how I now see SEO:

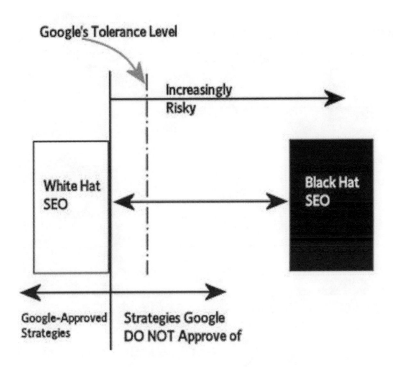

We've still got White Hat and Black Hat, but the connection between them is not as straight forward for the webmaster.

The "increasingly risky, increasingly safe" line that I drew in the first diagram (pre-Panda & Penguin) has now become the line that marks the approved and non-approved strategies boundary. This is now right up against the white hat boundary.

You'll notice that there is a new "Tolerance" lines drawn on the diagram. This tolerance line can move left to right, depending on how Google tweak their algorithm. If they want to come down hard on "spammers", they'll move the line to the left. If too many good sites get taken out as "collateral damage", they may move the tolerance line to the right a bit (although see the section later on "Trust v No-Trust"). Generally though, for most sites, the tolerance level is very close to the White hat boundary.

A webmaster that uses techniques which are further to the right than this approval line is risking their rankings.

Although these diagrams are good to work from, they do not display the whole truth.

Let's just consider the current state of SEO – the one post-Panda & Penguin.

Trust Vs no-trust

The Google Tolerance line will be in a different place depending on the site that is being ranked. For a site that has proven its worth and Google trusts a lot, we might see the diagram like this:

A trusted site

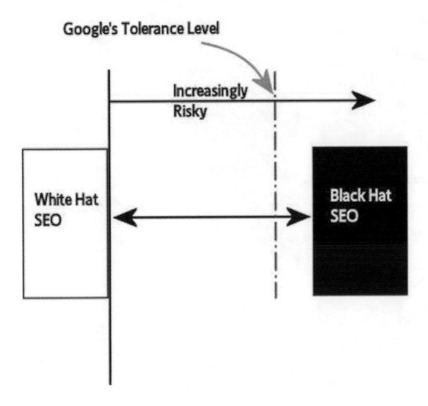

Yet for a new site, and one that has no track record to speak of, the diagram will probably look a lot more like this.

A non-trusted site

The only difference is in the location of the dashed "tolerance line".

In other words, Google are a lot more tolerant to sites that have built up authority and trust than they are to new sites, or sites that have not been able to attain a decent level of authority.

A high authority site with lots of trust can withstand a certain amount of spammy SEO without incurring a penalty (see later when we discuss "negative SEO"). The more authority, the more it can endure.

A new site on the other hand, would be quickly penalized for even a small amount of spammy SEO.

Webmasters living in the past

A lot of webmasters (or SEO companies vying for your business) may disagree with my take on modern-day SEO, and that's fine. The more people who just don't get it, the less competition there is for me and my clients.

I am sure you can find people that will say this is all rubbish and that they can get your pages ranked for your search terms (depending on the severity of competition of course), by heavily backlinking the page using keyword rich anchor text.

The process they'll describe is something like this:

1. Keyword research to find high demand, low competition phrases.
2. Create a page that is optimized for that keyword phrase.
3. Get lots of backlinks using that keyword phrase as anchor text.
4. Watch your page rise up the search engine results pages (SERPs).

If you don't care about your business, let them try. You might get short term gains, but you'll run the risk of losing all your rankings further down the line when Google catch up with you (and catch up they will... eventually).

To lose all of your rankings does not necessarily take a human review, though that can get your site penalized as well. No, getting your site penalized is far easier and the process Google has created is far more "automated" since the introduction of Panda and Penguin. Go over the threshold levels of what is acceptable, and the penalty is algorithmically determined and applied.

The good news is that algorithmic penalties can just as easily be lifted by removing the offending SEO and cleaning up your site. However, if that offending SEO includes low quality backlinks to your site (especially to the homepage), things are a little trickier.

Remember that SEO expert you hired that threw tens of thousands of backlinks at your site using his secret software? How can you get those backlinks removed? In many cases you can't, and moving the site to a new domain may be your only option.

In the rest of this book, I want to focus on what you need to do to help your pages rank better. I'll be focusing on purely white-hat strategies because black-hat is just not a long-term strategy. Remember, with the flick of a switch Google can change the goal posts again, leaving you out in the cold. Is it worth risking your business for short-term gains?

Before we go on to look at the 4 pillars of post-Penguin SEO, let's consider Hummingbird and where that fits into this puzzle.

Hummingbird – Another Animal in Google's Zoo

Hummingbird is the name given to Google's latest search algorithm (and completely replaces the old one). This is a major change to the way Google sorts through the information in its index and a change of this scale has probably not occurred for over a decade.

Think of it this way. Panda and Penguin were changes to parts of the old algorithm, whereas Hummingbird is a completely new algorithm, although it still uses components of the old algorithm.

The algorithm is basically the mathematical equation(s) used to determine the most relevant pages to return in the search results. The equation is built of over 200 components, things like PageRank and incoming links, etc.

Apparently the name Hummingbird was chosen because of how fast and accurate these birds are. Although a lot of webmasters won't agree, Google obviously assume that is what their search results are like.

Google wanted to introduce a major update to the algorithm because of the evolution in the way people use Google to search. An example Google have given is in "conversation search" where people can now speak into their mobile phone, tablet or even desktop browser to find information. Imagine you were interested in buying a Nexus 7 tablet. The old way of searching was to type something like this in the Google search box:

Buy Nexus 7

However, with speech, people have become a lot more descriptive in what they are search for. For example, it's easy to just dictate into your search browser something like:

"Where can I buy a Nexus 7 near here?"

The old Google could not cope as well with this second search phrase, but the new Hummingbird is designed to do just that. The old Google would look for pages in the index that included some or all of the words in the search phrase. A page that included the exact phrase would have the best chance of appearing at the top of Google. If no pages were found with the exact phrase, then Google would look for pages that included the important words from that phrase, e.g. "where" "buy" and "nexus 7".

The idea behind Hummingbird is that it should be able to interpret what the searcher is really looking for. In this case, they are clearly looking for somewhere near their current location that they can purchase a Nexus 7.

In other words, Hummingbird is suppose to determine searcher intent and return pages that best match that intent (as opposed to best matching keywords in the search phrase). Hummingbird tries to understand exactly what the searcher wants, rather than just taking into account the words used in the search term.

Today, in 2014 and beyond, optimizing for specific keyword phrases has not just become difficult (because of Panda & Penguin), it has become less effective in driving traffic if those phrases do not match the intent of the searcher typing those phrases into Google.

The 4 pillars of post-Penguin SEO

I have been doing SEO for around 10 years now and I have always concentrated on long-term strategies. That's not to say I haven't dabbled in black hat, because I have. However, almost without exception, all of the sites I promoted with black hat SEO have now been penalized. Since I don't want you to suffer the same fate with your website, I'll only be discussing white hat, safe techniques here.

I divide SEO strategies into four main areas. These are:

1. Quality content
2. Site organization
3. Authority
4. What's in it for the visitor?

These are the four areas where you need to concentrate your efforts. So let's now have a look at each of them in turn.

1. **Quality content**

Before we begin, let me just say that a lot of SEO "experts" have disagreed with me on the need for quality content as a major ranking factor. They will often cite exceptions in the search engines where pages rank well for competitive terms without any on-page content. The fact that these exceptions rarely last more than a week or two escapes them. However, I do like to answer my critics. If you are one of those people that questions the need for quality content, then I encourage you to watch a video I recorded before you read the rest of this book. You can watch the video here:

http://bit.ly/1c6YTRZ

BTW; those that agree with me about the need for quality content, or those on the fence, can also watch that video. It's quite an eye opener.

So let's get back to the idea of quality content, and what that means.

There are a number of different types of content that you can add to your site including articles, product reviews, quizzes, videos etc. However, no matter what type of content you are looking at, it has to:

1. Be created for the visitor, not the search engines. That means it needs to read well and have no visible signs of keyword phrases that have only been added to help the Page Rank better.
2. Add value to the top 10 SERPs (if you want to rank in the top 10, your page has to be seen as adding something unique to that collection of pages).
3. Give your visitors what they want.

   To put it simply, all of the content on your site has to be the best you can make it.

   A good rule of thumb I like to follow is this; would the content look out of place if it were published in a glossy magazine?

   If you hire ghostwriters, make sure you proof read the content to ensure that any **facts are correct** and there are **no spelling or grammar errors**.

   As you read through the content that you intend to post onto your website, ask yourself:

   • Is it content that your visitors will find useful?

   • Is there information in there that your visitors are unlikely to know, and therefore find informative?

• If it's a review, does it sound overly hyped up? Are both sides of the argument covered (i.e. positives and negatives)? Is there information in the review that is not available on the manufacturer's website or Amazon? Does the review offer a different way of looking at things which may help the buyer make a better informed decision prior to purchase?

To help us clarify what we see as quality content, let's take a look at some poor content.

Here is the first paragraph of an article I found online. Can you guess what **the** author was trying to optimize the page for?

Understanding Pomegranate Juice Benefits

Some people may not be that knowledgeable about pomegranate juice benefits but it is actually a very effective source of Vitamin C. The pomegranate fruit contains a lot of healthy nutrients and you can get a lot of good immune system boosters out of pomegranate juice benefits. It can actually provide around 16% of the required amount of Vitamin C that adults need to take on a daily basis. Pomegranate juice benefits also include Vitamin B5 as well as the antioxidant element of polyphenols and potassium.

The underlined keywords are part of the Kontera advertising system, so just ignore that.

It's not too difficult to guess the main phrase the author was targeting, is it?

"Pomegranate juice benefits" – it sticks out like a sore thumb. In fact, in a relatively short article (415 words) that phrase appeared 17 times. That's a density of 4%!

How many people think a density of 4% is OK or natural? Is repeating the same phrase 4 times every 100 words natural?

Let me tell you what a natural density is.

Ready for this….

It's **whatever density occurs naturally when an expert in their field writes an article**.

If you look back at that opening paragraph, there is an even bigger sin.

Here, look again:

Understanding Pomegranate Juice Benefits

Some people may not be that knowledgeable about pomegranate juice benefits but it is actually a very effective source of Vitamin C. The pomegranate fruit contains a lot of healthy nutrients and you can get a lot of good immune system boosters out of pomegranate juice benefits. It can actually provide around 16% of the required amount of Vitamin C that adults need to take on a daily basis. Pomegranate juice benefits also include Vitamin B5 as well as the antioxidant element of polyphenols and potassium.

Did you notice anything strange about that highlighted phrase?

It doesn't make sense, does it? This is a very clear indicator that the author was stuffing that phrase into the article in an attempt to help the article rank higher for that phrase.

You know, the sad thing is that this type of article may well have ranked well before Panda and Penguin. Why is that sad? Because web searchers had to put up with this kind of rubbish.

Today, no amount of sneaky black hat techniques could get this page into the top 10 (at least not for the long term). That is the difference between pre and post Panda/Penguin SEO.

If I actually do a search for "pomegranate juice benefits" in Google, the top ranked page (at the time of writing) included the exact phrase ONCE in an article of over 1000 words in length. That's a density of 0.1%.

OK, so the first lesson to learn – throw keyword density rules out of the window.

What may be a surprise to many, is that out of the top 10 pages ranking for the term "pomegranate juice benefits", only THREE have that phrase in the page title. In fact, **only three of the top 10** pages actually include that phrase anywhere in the article.

Perhaps you think that statistic is just a fluke?

Try it with any search term that isn't a brand name or product name. In general, the top 10 search results in Google list far fewer pages containing the actual search term (although this does seem to fluctuate somewhat as Google twiddle their algorithm "dials").

So just how is Google able to decide on how to rank webpages for the term "pomegranate juice benefits" (or any other search term), if they are not looking for that actual phrase in the content?

The answer to that lies in the words on the page. Let me ask you a question.

Does your article sound as if it was written by an expert?

The reason I ask is because when an article is written by somebody who really knows their subject, they will use a certain "niche vocabulary". That is, they will use words and phrases that actually define the topic of the article.

You can read an article I wrote on this called "Niche Vocabulary - why poor content can't hide in Google". You will see in that article, that if your content does not contain its niche vocabulary, you're very unlikely to rank in Google for the long term.

Every article you write will have its own niche vocabulary.

Two articles on a similar topic will share a percentage of that niche vocabulary, but not all of it will be shared.

Let's take the same example used in articles on epilepsy, and have a look at how the pages in Google use their niche vocabulary.

To carry out a test, I found a number of words on the top 10 pages of Google ranking for the term epilepsy using Web Content Studio. These words appeared on many of the top 10 pages ranking for that term. These are what I call theme words (or niche vocabulary), i.e. words that commonly appear in articles that are written on a given topic.

Here are the theme words I found for the term epilepsy:

age, aid, anti, brain, cause, children, control, develop, diagnosis, diet, doctor, drugs, epilepsy, epileptic, guide, health, help, home, information, ketogenic, life, living, log, medical, medications, part, plan, research, seizure, seizure-free, seizures, side, special, support, surgery, symptoms, take, term, test, time, treatment, types, unit, work

What I would like to do is check a couple of different epilepsy "sub-niches" to see if these words appear. The sub niches are:

1. Epilepsy treatment
2. Ketogenic diet

Both of these terms are highly related to epilepsy (the ketogenic diet is a diet that helps cure epilepsy in a number of patients). Since they are both talking about epilepsy, they both should contain a lot of the epilepsy niche vocabulary.

First let's have a look at the top ranking pages for the term **epilepsy**. Here is a screenshot showing the number one ranked article with the theme words I found earlier highlighted in yellow (light highlights):

isturbed **brain** activity that **cause** changes in attention or behavior. se
ses, incidence, and risk factors **epilepsy** occurs when permanent cha
e **cause** the **brain** to be too excitable or jumpy. the **brain** sends out
als. this results in repeated, unpredictable **seizures**. (a single **seizure**
pen again is not **epilepsy**.) **epilepsy** may be due to a **medical** condit
affects the **brain**, or the **cause** may be unknown (idiopathic). comm
epsy include: stroke or transient ischemic attack (tia) dementia, such
ase traumatic **brain** injury infections, including **brain** abscess, mening
aids brain problems that are present at birth (congenital **brain** defec
occurs during or near bith metabolism disorders that a child may be t
henylketonuria) **brain** tumor abnormal blood vessels in the **brain** oth
age or destroy **brain** tissue **epilepsy seizures** usually begin betwee
but they can happen at any **age**. there may be a family history of **seiz**
epsy. symptoms symptoms vary from person to person. some peo
le staring spells, while others have violent shaking and loss of alertne:
ure depends on the **part of the brain** affected and **cause** of epileps
a the seizure is similar to the previous one, some people with epilep

You can only see a small section of the article here, as it's quite long, but I'm sure you'll agree
that the theme words are well sprinkled throughout.

Let's repeat this but using the number one ranked article for the term **epilepsy treatment**:

with the introduction of dilantin (warner-lambert), has been a triumph of mode
e. the **development of newer medications**, especially tegretol (ciba-geigy) an
reckitt & colman) has meant that **epilepsy** can be suppressed in most patients
serious or annoying **side effects**. this is not to say that every patient can be full
lled, or that **side** effects do not occur. a continuing effort is being made by
ional pharmaceutical companies to find safer, more effective **treatment**
sy. new **drugs** are not cascading onto the market however, for the high cost of
ch, **development** and marketing (about a$150 million for any new drug) is an
int disincentive. how do **drugs** prevent **seizures**? strange to say, most of the
used in treating **epilepsy** today were discovered to have **anti-epileptic** proper
ice. we have used these **drugs** with great benefit for years without really knowi
ey **work**. however, a more systematic search for new **anti-epileptic** s is n
vay, based on **research** progress in understanding how neurones transmit
:s to each other, and our increasing knowledge of the structure and function of tl
ane which surrounds each neurone. the messages that one neurone sends to the
editated by releasing neurotransmitter chemicals, can either excite the neurone
line, or can inhibit its electrical activity. the identification of gamaa-amino butyric

Once again we see the theme words sprinkled throughout the content as we would expect,
since this article is also about epilepsy.

Let's now look at the final example, which is the **ketogenic diet**:

15

ketogenic diet was then gradually forgotten as new **anticonvulsant medications** developed. the **ketogenic diet** has recently been 'rediscovered' and is achieving increasingly widespread use. its modern day role as alternative management for ch with difficult-to-**control epilepsy** is currently being re-defined. the ketogenic die a 'fad' or a 'quack **diet**', but rather is an alternative **medical treatment** childr difficult-to-**control epilepsy**. the **ketogenic diet** should only be used under the supervision of a physician and a **dietician**. background fasting to achieve **control seizure** was described in both the bible and during the middle **ages**, but it was o during the early 1920s that scientific papers first appeared describing the beneficia effects of prolonged fasting for **children** whose **epilepsy** could not be **controlled** few **medications** then available. these papers claimed that starvation, drinking onl for 10 to 20 or more days, could result in **control** **seizure** for prolonged peric **time**. during this era, when the metabolic effects of diabetes were also being studi was noted that the biochemical effects of fasting could be mimicked by eating a di

This too has the theme words for epilepsy sprinkled throughout.

Since all of these articles have epilepsy theme words sprinkled throughout them, they could all theoretically rank for the term epilepsy, but the most important thing is that Google will know the article is about epilepsy because they contain epilepsy-related words and phrases.

Each of these articles actually has **a slightly different set of theme words** which help to define what area of epilepsy they are discussing. We could show this by finding theme words specific to each of the three articles and we would see they were different (though there would be a core of epilepsy related words).

However, let's try something a little different. Let's look at a second test.

Test 2 - I found a number of "theme phrases" – 2, 3 & 4 word phrases that are common to the top 10 ranked pages for the three terms – epilepsy treatment, ketogenic diet & epilepsy.

I pooled all of these phrases together and then checked the top three ranking pages for epilepsy, epilepsy treatment, and the ketogenic diet.

If each article has a slightly different niche vocabulary, then we should see different theme phrases being used in each of the articles. Let's have a look at the epilepsy article first:

have simple staring spells, while others have violent shaking and loss
ness. the type of seizure depends on the ███████████ affected
cause of epilepsy. most of the time, the seizure is similar to the previor
some people with epilepsy have a strange sensation (such as tingling,
ling an odor that isn't actually there, or emotional changes) before eac
ire. this is called an aura. for a detailed description of the symptoms
ciated with a specific type of seizure, see: absence (petit mal) seizure
ralized tonic-clonic (grand mal) seizure partial (focal) seizure signs an
the doctor will perform a physical exam, which will include a detailed
at the brain and nervous system. an eeg (electroencephalogram) will
one to check the electrical ████████████ people with epileps
 often have abnormal electrical activity seen on this test. in some cases,
est may show the area in the brain where the seizures start. the brain
appear normal after a seizure or between seizures. to diagnose
psy or plan for ████████████ you may need to wear an eeg

The phrases are marked in black. You cannot see the actual phrases in the screenshots, and that is unimportant. I'll list them below. Just note for now that they are dispersed in the article.

Here is a list of theme phrases found in the epilepsy article:

activity in the brain
atkins diet
blood sugar
causes of epilepsy
epilepsy medication
epilepsy medications
epilepsy surgery
ketogenic diet
part of the brain
seizure medicines
temporal lobe
vagus nerve

Let's repeat the test using the top ranking article for epilepsy treatment:

ketogenic diet to treat epilepsy. once started on anti-epileptic medication never stop it unless advised to do so by a doctor. stopping medication on one's own is likely to produce a series of major seizures, a dangerous condition. back to **treatment of epilepsy** which drug to use the choice of drug depends on: the type of epilepsy. some drugs such as epilim are activ in a wide range of seizures (tonic-clonic, absence attacks, etc.) while zarontin, for example, is active only against absence seizures. possible side effects. for example, dilantin tends to promote hair growth on the body an face, and should be avoided in women of dark complexion. dilantin also seems more likely to produce slowing of thought processes including memory than the newer anticonvulsant such as tegretol or epilim, which do not usually produce these symptoms. anticipation of pregnancy. all **anti epileptic drug**s carry a small risk to the unborn child. we will consider this

Here are the theme phrases on the top ranked page for epilepsy treatment:

adverse effects
aid for seizures
anticonvulsant drug
anticonvulsant drugs
anti-epileptic drug
anti-epileptic medications
anti-seizure medications
controlling seizures
epileptic control
epileptic seizures
ketogenic diet
seizure control
seizure medications
temporal lobe
treatment of epilepsy
treatments for epilepsy

And finally for the phrase "ketogenic diet", here are the theme phrases:

last updated 16 sep 2010, review date due 16 sep 2011 the ████████
███ is a ███████, adequate protein, low carbohydrate diet designed to
mimic many of the biochemical changes associated with prolonged
starvation. first developed in the early 1900s, and successfully used for the
██████████████s in children during the 20s and 30s, the ████████
███ was then gradually forgotten as new anticonvulsant medications were
developed. the ████████████ has recently been 'rediscovered' and is
achieving increasingly widespread use. its modern day role as alternative
management for children with difficult-to-control epilepsy is currently being
re-defined. the ████████████ is not a 'fad' or a 'quack diet', but rather is
an alternative ████████████████████ with difficult-to-control
epilepsy. the ████████████ should only be used under the supervision of
a physician and a dietician. background fasting to achieve ████████
████████ was described in both the bible and during the middle ages, but it

These are the phrases found:

anticonvulsant drug
anticonvulsant drugs
beta hydroxybutyric acid
body fat
control of seizures
control seizures
diet controls seizures
different anticonvulsants
high fat
high fat diet
high fat intake
medical treatment for children
protein and carbohydrate
seizure control
seizure type
treatment of seizure
while on the diet
Let's compare the theme phrases of these three articles in a table:

Epilepsy	Epilepsy Treatment	Ketogenic Diet
activity in the brain	adverse effects	anticonvulsant drug
atkins diet	aid for seizures	anticonvulsant drugs
blood sugar	anticonvulsant drug	beta hydroxybutyric acid
causes of epilepsy	anticonvulsant drugs	body fat
epilepsy medication	anti-epileptic drug	control of seizures
epilepsy medications	anti-epileptic	control seizures
epilepsy surgery	medications	diet controls seizures
ketogenic diet	anti-seizure	different anticonvulsants
part of the brain	medications	high fat
seizure medicines	controlling seizures	high fat diet
temporal lobe	epileptic control	high fat intake
vagus nerve	epileptic seizures	medical treatment for children
	ketogenic diet	protein and carbohydrate
	seizure control	seizure control
	seizure medications	seizure type
	temporal lobe	treatment of seizure
	treatment of epilepsy	while on the diet
	treatments for epilepsy	

This table clearly shows that each of the three articles have a different niche vocabulary.

As we saw above, all three articles have theme words relating to epilepsy as we would expect. However each of the articles also had their own set of theme phrases which help to distinguish the actual sub-niche within epilepsy.

The **epilepsy** article has a wide range of theme phrases relating to all aspects of epilepsy.

The **epilepsy treatment** article focused more on phrases that are related to the treatment of epilepsy (big surprise eh?).

The **ketogenic diet** article had more theme phrases relating to the diet itself and the control seizures.

How can you use this information to write better content?

If you are an expert in the field you are writing about, you will automatically and naturally use these theme words and phrases as you write about the topic. The truth is that you need to use these theme words and phrases if your article is to make sense and look authoritative.

If however you are not an expert, then things are a little more difficult. You need to find which words and phrases are important to the topic you want to write about.

As you write the content sprinkle in theme words (that are single words that are highly related to the niche). This will help the search engines to identify the topic. Also pick a small number of highly relevant theme phrases (2, 3 and 4+ word phrases) and include these in your content (once is enough but write for the visitor, so use theme words and phrases when you need to).

These theme phrases should be the most important ones that relate to the niche and will leave the search engines in no doubt about the topic. Do not under any circumstances use theme words or phrases that are not necessary. E.g. don't just repeat a phrase 3 or 4 times in the content because you want that page to rank for that term. Google's Penguin will be onto you and you could find your rankings drop for keyword stuffing or unnatural use of keywords.

Below is an example of a badly written article where theme phrases have been repeated solely for search engines. Here is the first half of an article. Ignoring the quality of the information in this piece, let's just look at an example of keyword stuffing:

DIY Architecture

Let's say you are planning a room addition. Did you know that you already possess the talents which allow you to calculate a comfortable size for the room addition? You may even possess some good design skills. Now you might think that I am wrong on this one.

For sake of discussion, let's assume that your local zoning ordinances will permit you to do just about anything. Some cities have strict setback lines and so forth that may limit the size of your planned addition - you must be aware of these limitations.

Go into your present living room. How does it feel? Imagine if it were say 6 feet wider and 8 feet longer. Maybe this size would allow you the space for that new couch, or a fireplace, built-in bookcases, whatever. The point is this. Use your existing rooms as starting points. You can measure them and stretch them to suit your needs. You need to start thinking in terms of space and how much you need.

Putting it on Paper

Remember earlier how I told you that my drafting skills were poor. Today, you don't need to know how to draw! If you have a fairly modern computer and sufficient memory, there are many affordable computer design programs that will draw your planned room addition.

I have highlighted one phrase that occurs three times (but I could have chosen a different example in this same article). The phrase is "room addition" and to me it sticks out because it is actually a little awkward to read, even unnatural when you read the text around the phrase (which is fluff and padding). When that happens, I assume that the webmaster included the term for the search engines, and if we check Google Keyword Tool, we can get a fairly strong confirmation of that:

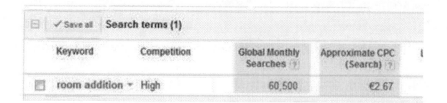

	Keyword	Competition	Global Monthly Searches ?	Approximate CPC (Search) ?	
☐	room addition ▾	High	60,500	€2.67	

That phrase has 60,500 monthly searches, and costs advertisers around 2.67 Euros PER CLICK. With the AdSense ads on this site, that phrases could well have been a nice little earner.

Funnily enough, the site where this article is found used to be a site that Google showed off as a quality AdSense/Affiliate website. In the recent rounds of Panda and Penguin updates, this site was penalized. This caused a lot of webmasters to conclude that Google does not like affiliate sites. After all, an affiliate site that Google once showcased as a shining example was itself penalized.

My view on this is that Google simply does not like poor or spammy content. This particular site was probably lucky to get away with its content for as long as it did, and most probably never got a real in-depth human review. When Google introduced the Panda and Penguin updates, these largely automated pieces of code caught the site and identified much of its content as low quality and in violation of the Google guidelines. On looking through a lot of the earlier content on that site, I'd agree that it was penalized for good reason.

2. Site organization

A note about Exact Match Domain names

An exact match domain (EMD) is one that is basically using the main keyword phrase you are targeting as the domain name, e.g. buyviagraonline.com (if you wanted to target "buy Viagra online"). Typically, EMD websites target very few keywords, with all eggs being placed firmly in the "EMD phrase" basket.

If you are starting a new website, choosing a domain will be the first task you'll need to do. Many people who teach SEO will tell you to go for an EMD because it offers ranking advantages over non-EMDs. This was true in the past, but less so now. In fact, on September 28th 2012, Google released an update that was meant to reduce the ranking ability of poor quality EMDs. You can read the announcement by Matt Cutts (Google's head of spam) on Twitter here. This shouldn't really have come as a surprise to the better SEOs, because Matt Cutts announced that Google would be looking at why EMDs ranked so well when he spoke at Pubcon in November 2010 (2 years ago).

The problem with EMDs now is that they are scrutinized by Google. It will probably take a lot less to get an EMD site penalized nowadays; therefore I recommend you look for a brandable domain name instead. Find a domain name that people will remember.

What is a low quality EMD?

I would say that any EMD that is not a brand or company name is at risk of being labeled low quality. The reason is simply that EMDs are chosen by webmasters to rank for a particular phrase.

Webmasters have traditionally looked at their keyword research, found a phrase that is commercially attractive (low competition, high search volume, high AdWords Cost per click) and registered the phrase as an EMD with the intention of ranking for that phrase and monetizing with Google AdSense. Any website that is setup with the primary goal of ranking for a single phrase is likely to be low quality in the eyes of the search engines; after all, websites are there to display quality information on topics, not single phrases.

One thing that makes a lot of these low quality EMDs stand out is the high percentage of backlinks that use the exact same keyword phrase as anchor text. The problem for EMD owners is that using that phrase is natural, because it's the name of the website. This is why I suggest you avoid them, unless it is your company/brand name.

Summary: Any EMD that has obviously been chosen solely for it potential profit is likely to have problems going forward.

Site structure

The way you structure your site is extremely important not only for the search engines but also human visitors. Good organization coupled with a clear and intuitive navigation system is vital.

From a human point of view, it makes sense that content on a similar topic should all be found in the same section of the site. For example, if you have a website selling bicycles, all of the mountain bikes should be found together, all of the road bikes in another section, and maybe bikes for children in another section.

If a 22 year old mountain bike rider came to your site, she should be able to browse the mountain bike stuff without seeing road racers or children's bicycles.

If you're using WordPress as a site builder, organizing your site like this is extremely easy. You simply create a category for each section and assign that category to relevant posts as you publish them. I tend to only assign one category to every post as this makes for a tighter organization (a better silo). If I need to further categorize the articles, e.g. having all 26 inch frame bikes on the same page, I'd use tags instead of categories for the frame sizes. We'll look at tags a little later.

This type of "silo" structure works very well for the search engines as well because it helps them categorize your content. Think of the site that has reviews on the following bikes and accessories.

• Allen Deluxe 4-Bike Hitch Mount Rack

• GMC Denali Pro Road Bike

• GMC Denali Women's Road Bike

• GMC Topkick Dual-Suspension Mountain Bike

• Hollywood Racks E3 Express 3-Bike Trunk Mount Rack

• Kawasaki DX226FS 26-Inch Dual Suspension Mountain Bike

• Mongoose Exile Dual-Suspension Mountain Bike

• Pacific Stratus Men's Mountain Bike

• Topeak Explorer Bike Rack

• Victory Vision Men's Road Bike

If you were to put them into related group (silos), those silos would look something like this.

Silo 1 Mountain Bikes

GMC Topkick Dual-Suspension Mountain Bike

Kawasaki DX226FS 26-Inch Dual Suspension Mountain Bike

Mongoose Exile Dual-Suspension Mountain Bike

Pacific Stratus Men's Mountain Bike

Silo 2 Road Bikes

GMC Denali Pro Road Bike

GMC Denali Women's Road Bike

Victory Vision Men's Road Bike

Silo 3 Car Racks

Allen Deluxe 4-Bike Hitch Mount Rack

Hollywood Racks E3 Express 3-Bike Trunk Mount Rack

Topeak Explorer Bike Rack

So overall then, the structure of our site would be as follows:

Internal links

One of the most overlooked pieces of the SEO puzzle is internal linking.   This not only helps the search engines spider your pages, but it also helps visitors find other related content within your site.

With WordPress, there are plugins that can help you automate some of the internal linking on your site. For example "Yet Another Related Posts" plugin, or YARP to its friends, is a free WordPress plugin that will automatically create a related posts section at the end of every article on your site. You can configure it so that it can only find related posts within the same category if you want and this can help create a tighter, more natural silo with articles linking out to related content on your site.

Here is an example of a "Related Posts" section from a post on one of my own websites:

Related Articles

- Top 12 WordPress Plugins For WordPress 2.7.x - Here is my top 12 V 2.7.x Bookmark on DeliciousDigg this postRecommend on Facebook with StumblersTweet about itBuzz it upSubscribe to the comments on

- Top 10 WordPress Plugins - NOTE: This article is quite old. On 10th I with an update of what plugins I use. The article is Top 12 WordPres WordPress Plugins. I do use others, but these are the first ones I ins WordPress site. 1.

- Best WordPress Ratings & Review Plugin? - WordPress is a fantastic with a ratings and review plugin, your visitors can actually add value to ratings and reviews of products. I tested out 4 WordPress Ratings & F winner. Bookmark on DeliciousDigg this postRecommend on Facebc

There are a number of "related posts" plugins that you can use to achieve the same thing.

Linking pages together

Another form of internal linking, which I think is extremely important, is links within the body of your articles.

For example, if you are writing an article about the "GMC Topkick Dual-Suspension Mountain Bike", you might like to compare certain features of the bike to the "Mongoose Exile Dual-Suspension Mountain Bike". When you mention the name of the Mongoose Exile bike, it would help your visitors if you linked that phrase to your Mongoose Exile review. This would also help the search engines to find that article, and help them determine what it is about (based on the link text).

This type of internal linking helps to increase indexing of your site as well as the rankings of individual pages.

To read more about internal linking between pages on your site, I recommend you read an article that I wrote on the subject called "Internal Linking & SEO".

Tags - another way to categorize your content

Tags are another way to categorize content if you are running a WordPress site. When you write a post, you can include a number of these tags which can help further categorize the piece.

For example, if you wrote a post about the "Dyson DC 33 Animal" vacuum, you would probably put it in the category "Dyson" as that is the most logical "navigation label" for your visitors.

However, you might also want to allow visitors to easily find vacuums that use the Dyson Ball technology, or contain a HEPA filter. Rather than have a category for "Dyson Ball" and "HEPA filter" and then put that DC33 animal in all three categories, a better way would be to create tags for this extra classification.

For example, here are some tags you might use on your vacuum site:

• Upright

• Dyson Ball

• Pet hair

• HEPA filter

• Bagless

These tags will help to categorize the posts within the Dyson category (and every other category on your site).

WordPress actually creates a page for each of these tags and each of these tag pages can actually rank quite well in Google.

Let's use look at an example.

These four vacuums all have a HEPA filter:

1. Eureka Boss Smart-Vac Upright.
2. Hoover Windtunnel
3. BISSELL Cleanview Helix Upright Vacuum Cleaner
4. Miele S2 Series Lightweight

The first vacuum will be in the Eureka CATEGORY with all other Eureka vacuums.

The second vacuum will be in the Hoover CATEGORY with all other Hoover vacuums.

The third vacuum will be in the Bissell CATEGORY with all other Bissell vacuums.

The fourth vacuum will be in the Miele CATEGORY with all other Miele vacuums.

However, all 4 vacuums would also appear on the HEPA Filter "tag page".

In addition, the first three would all appear on the "Upright" tag page with all other upright vacuums.

When people visit your site, they'll be able to narrow down their choice by Brand (using category navigation), or by looking for specific features (using Tags to navigate).

WARNING

I advise that you use tags wisely. Don't tag every post with hundreds of tags. Think about your tags and only include the most relevant ones for each post.

Use and abuse of tags

A lot of people do not really understand the significance of tags, and see them as a "keyword list" much like the "vestigial" keyword Meta tag. To that end, they create long tag lists for each post. Here is a screenshot of some tags assigned to one post I saw:

Tags: advantages disadvantages of solar power, advantages of a solar panels, advantages of solar cell panel, are MONOCRYSTALLINE sollar pannels good, best mono solar panel price, best quality monocrystaline solar panels, bestpv panels mono or poly, buy pv panels monocrystalline, compare monocrystalin policrystalin photovoltaic, compare monocrystalline and polycrystalline, compare monocrystalline and polycrystalline pannel, compare pollycrystalline vs. monocrystalline modules, crystal cells for solar panels, crystal solar, crystalline si solar efficiency, crystalline solar best, crystalline solar cell technology, crystalline solar cells cost, crystalline solar panels, crystalline solar plate cost, crystalline solar pv module, csun mono-crystalline panels, describe 2 advantages of solar cells, difference between mono and polycrystalline, difference between monocrystalline, difference monocrystalline polycrystalline solar, difference solar panels polycrystalline &, disadvantage to many solar panels, ecokes monocrystalline, ecokes photovoltaic panels, ecokes solar panel, electricity, energy, how i get Monocrystalline silicon, how many rating monocrystalline cell, how Monocrystalline cells are made, how to produce monocrytaline silicon, http://www.monocrystal photo cells/, is monocrystalline better than polycrystalline, is monocrystalline PV best, LUXOR Solar Mono Crystal Dickschichtmodule, maker of monocrystalline panels, mon vs poly efficiency, mono and poly crystalline, mono crystalline pv panels, mono or poly solar panels, mono silicon solar panels, mono solar panel dimensions, mono solar power, mono v poly solar panels, mono versus poly crystalling panels, mono vs poly crystalline panels, mono vs. multicrystalline solar panel, Mono-Crystalline & Poly crystalline, mono-crystalline cells vs poly, mono-crystalline efficiency rating, Mono-Crystalline or Polycrystalline solar panel, Mono-crystalline pv solar

They just keep scrolling down the page. What you see in that list is just one QUARTER of the tags listed for that particular post.

In SEO terms, this is bad practice, very bad!

To understand why long tag lists is generally a bad idea, let's look what happens when you create a post.

When you make a post on your blog, WordPress will try to put the post on several pages of your site including:

1. A page specially created to show the post

2. The category page

3. On every tag page

4. On the author page

   Can you see how that one post can be duplicated on multiple pages of your site?

   Duplicate content on a site is NOT a good thing!

   Let's consider now the tag pages that are created when you make a post.

   If you have 50 tags assigned to a post, that article will be posted 50+ times on your blog (on 50 different tag pages plus the other pages mentioned above).

   Another big problem with using lots of tags occurs when a particular tag is only used for one post. In that case, the tag page will only have the one article on it, meaning it is almost identical to the post page created by WordPress for that article.

How to use WordPress tags properly

Get into the tag mindset!

Before you use a tag on a post, think in terms of a page being created for each tag you use. Your article will appear on each of those tag pages. Is that what you want? Is this tag going to be used on other relevant posts? Never use a tag if it will not be used by several other posts on your site.

With this in mind, here is what I suggest you do:

During the design stages of your site, make a list on a piece of paper of all the tags you want to use on your site (you can add/edit this list as you build out your site, but have a list you can refer to). These will be the most important keywords for the niche, but they should be keywords that are different to the categories you have set up for the site (never use a tag that is also a category name). After all, WordPress will create pages for each category anyway; so think of tags as an "additional" categorization tool at your disposal.

As you create posts on your site, refer to the tag list you wrote down, and use only tags on that list. By all means add new tags over time, but make sure that tags are going to be used more than once. Don't create a tag that will only ever be used on a single post on your site. Also, only use a few of the most relevant tags for each post.

What if my site already has a lot of posts with spammy tags?

Fortunately there are a number of good plugins to help manage tags if you work with WordPress. Just visit the Plugin directory and search for "Simple Tags". That's one that does a good job in allowing you to modify and edit your tass. Use it to clean up your site.

Modifying tag pages?

Quite often you'll find that your tag pages are getting traffic from Google. I have found that the tag pages often rank very well for the chosen tag (as a keyword phrase).

I like to modify my tag pages so that I can add an introductory section to each one. However, this requires some knowledge of templates, which is beyond the scope of this book.

The tag page I end up with has an article/introduction, followed by a list of all related articles (those which have been tagged with that particular tag). This helps make your tag pages unique, but also allows you to add more value to your site.

Used properly, tag pages can work for you. Used without thought, tag pages can increase duplicate content on your site and increase your chances of getting penalized by Google.

3. Authority

Here is a question for you:

What is an Authority Site?

If you go over to the Free Dictionary website and search for authority, there are a lot of different definitions. This definition is probably most apt with regards to websites:

au·thor·i·ty (ə-thôr'ĭ-tē, ə-thŏr'-, ô-thôr'-, ô-thŏr'-)
n. pl. **au·thor·i·ties**
1.
    a. The power to enforce laws, exact obedience, command, determine, or judge.
    b. One that is invested with this power, especially a government or body of government officials: *land titles issued by the civil authority.*
2. Power assigned to another; authorization: *Deputies were given authority to make arrests.*
3. A public agency or corporation with administrative powers in a specified field: *a city transit authority.*
4.
    a. An accepted source of expert information or advice: *a noted authority on birds; a reference book often cited as an authority.*
    b. A quotation or citation from such a source: *biblical authorities for a moral argument.*

So to make your website be seen as an authority site by the search engines, it has to be an **"accepted source of expert information or advice"**.

That obviously starts with creating a well-optimized site filled with fantastic content (the first two pillars of good SEO that we have talked about). However, alone those two pillars are not enough to make your site an authority, because no-one will have heard about you or your great site.

Your site (or your own name if YOU personally want to be the authority) MUST be well-known in your particular niche.

So how do you get well known?

Well that's the easy part – *you need to put your site name and face out there on as many relevant, high quality places as you can, with links pointing back to relevant pages on your site*.

This all comes down to getting backlinks to your site, but it is also the area that can quickly get you penalized, especially if your site is relatively new or doesn't have much authority yet.

There is another aspect of this I want to discuss before we look deeper at back-linking, and that is linking out from your site to authority sites in your niche.

Think about it for a minute.

We are all part of a huge web of interlinked websites. If you were talking about something in your niche, doesn't it make sense that you might make references to other authority sites?

e.g. If a search engine was trying to evaluate your page on the Atkins Diet, don't you think that links to other peoples studies on the diet, as well as medical references, etc. would help make your page more of an authority? Sure it would, as long as your own content was also excellent. It would also help instill confidence in your visitor by giving them more value.

So when you are writing content for your website, don't be afraid to link to other authority sites if they have relevant information. Don't even use NOFOLLOW links, as that just tells the search engine that you:

(a) Don't trust the site you are linking to, or
(b) You are trying to hoard Page Rank to your own site.

I do recommend though that you open these links in a new window so that your visitors are not taken away from your site if they click these links. What you may even decide to do is have a reference section at the end of your content, with active hyperlinks pointing to other authority sites.

In short, link out to other authority sites - but only when it makes sense and you think it will help **your visitor**.

OK, outbound links are sorted.

What about the links coming into your site?

Backlinks to a website are still hugely important in the ranking of a webpage in Google. It's the main reason webmasters build links to their own websites – to help them rank better. However, there is something very important that you need to know about link building. It's not something that most SEO book or courses will tell you, mainly because they want to sell you their link building tools, or get you to buy recommended tools through their affiliate links. It's this:

Google don't want you building links to your site.

In fact, we can probably state it a little more strongly than that.

Google hate you building links to your site.

In fact, let's take it one step further.

If Google find links that you have created to your site, with the sole purpose of helping your site rank better, they will ignore those links at best, or penalise your site at worst.

Google are on the warpath against "webspam" and "link schemes", and that includes links that webmasters build to their own sites to help those sites rank better.

You need to bear this in mind as you build links to your web pages. Also, just because some SEO guru can show you that incoming anchor text rich links help a page rank better today, it does not mean that this "technique" will work tomorrow. A lot of what is taught in books and courses on SEO are dangerous for the long term. What I cover in this book is what I consider to be the best long-term strategy for link building, and one that doesn't look too unnatural to Google.

OK, let's look at the general concept of link building:

Search Rankings Increase

As you build quality links to your page, your page will move up the search engine rankings.

Some people will tell you that it doesn't matter whether inbound links are on pages which are highly related to your site or not, but that just doesn't make too much sense. And with Penguin and Panda quick to penalize, I recommend you ALWAYS consider quality in every backlink you get. That means quality of the page that your link is on (look to get links on authority sites), and quality of the content on the page your link is on.

NOTE: Having backlinks on pages/sites in a different niche to your own DID once work. However, that has all changed with Panda and Penguin.

Think about it logically.

If you had a website on "breeding goldfish", and you had 100 inbound links to your site but 95% of those were on pages that talked about things like:

• Prescription drugs

• Viagra

• Auto maintenance

• Wedding speeches

• Golf Equipment

• Etc

What is that telling the search engines?

I think that Google would look at these backlinks and decide that you were involved in backlinking strategies with the sole purpose or ranking better. Do you think they'd look favorably at that? No, and their quality guidelines say so.

If the search engines want to use inbound links as a measure of authority, then surely the most authoritative links you could get would be from quality pages that were on a similar topic to the page they link to?

With Google Penguin, this may be even more important as Google appears to be giving less weight to the anchor text and more to the actual THEME of the webpage (or site) that the link is on. Therefore, look for links from pages and sites that are relevant to your own, and look for quality sites to get your links on.

Is Negative SEO real?

Negative SEO is a relatively new term that refers to webmasters/SEOs who build poor quality links to their competitor's website to get it penalized. Many SEOs agree now that since Penguin, negative SEO is a reality. I actually think it was a reality even before Panda.

Before we look at negative SEO, and how it might work, let's look back over the last couple of years.

When Google released the Panda Updates in 2011, a lot of people complained that Google was targeting affiliate sites simply because their site got dropped, or lost serious rankings. My take on this is not that Google hates affiliates, but Google hates poor content and many affiliate sites were poor content. Most affiliate sites I have seen break so many of the Google guidelines that it does not surprise me they got hit. They have poor content and engage in dodgy link schemes.

In the past we all assumed that backlinking could not hurt us. If it could, then a competitor could simply bring your site down by creating lots of spammy backlinks.

I had a site that was several years old and a PR2.

Around the beginning of the 2011 (before Panda) I started some aggressive backlinking. I wanted to use this as a test so I set up about 150 blogs that I could use to get backlinks. I wanted to use blogs that I controlled so I could delete all backlinks if I needed to.

I started submitting content to these 150 sites, with backlinks going back to the pages on my test site.

For several weeks, the rankings climbed, and so did my traffic. I was monitoring 85 keywords, and around 60 had reached the top 10 in Google, with a large proportion in the top 3.

My site then got penalized. All 85 keywords dropped out of the top 100.

They stayed out of the top 100 for 8 weeks. I then started phase two of my test. I deleted all 150 blogs, thereby eliminating all of those spammy backlinks.

Over the next month, things started to improve slowly. Pages started climbing back into the top 100 to the point where I ended up with 64 of the 85 phrases back in the top 100. Around 42 pages were back in the top 30, and 12 were back in the top 10.

NOTE: Obviously my rankings did not return to pre-penalty levels, because they were only at those pre-penalty levels because of the backlinks I had built. However, I think it was fairly clear that my site penalty had been lifted.

So was it coincidence, or did those dodgy, poor quality backlinks really cause my site to be dropped? I have no proof either way, but from what I am hearing, the quality of inbound links may well affect rankings/penalties. This seems totally against what Matt Cutts of Google has told us in the past, but I believe it to be true.

You can read more about this if you are interested by searching Google for "negative SEO".

Let's take a look at how this might work. Here is a diagram:

Search Rankings
DECREASE

In this model, poor backlinks actually cause YOUR page to get penalized and drop down the rankings.

We'll revisit this diagram later in the book when we consider the implications of negative SEO to the way we backlink our backlinks.

The point to take home from this is to get backlinks from good authority sites. If possible, get links within the body of a quality article on the page that is linking to you. I realize that is not always possible, but on many sites you can.

What type of backlinks?

First and foremost, go for QUALITY, not quantity.

To be seen as a real authority, your site needs incoming links from other authority sites. Since Google Penguin, I no longer recommend using any type of automated link building tool.

WHAT?????

I know, I know....

"If I cannot use automated link building tools, how can I get enough links to rank well?"

To answer that question, let me ask you one thing.

Do you believe your page DESERVES to rank well based on the **quality of the content** and the **authority of you/your site**?

If you answer no, then you will have to go down the black hat SEO path to get your page ranked, and ultimately that path will lead to penalties and lost rankings.

For a page to rank well on your site, you need to make sure it **deserves** to rank well (in terms of content and your site/author authority).

Think of this example.

You write a page on the "health benefits of vitamin D".

Do you think your page deserves to rank above medical sites, where the authors are medical doctors? Why? Google clearly wants to show the most useful and accurate information it can to its visitors, and that probably means choosing a medical authority site over yours, even if your content is better. The problem is that you cannot compete on the authority level unless you are an authority on the "health benefits of vitamin D" and that is the way it should be.

How might you gain authority in this area? Well quite simply, you could write articles on vitamin D and have them posted on numerous authority sites, with a link back to your site/page. If you make use of Google's author attribution (it essentially means linking your content to your Google+ profile), which I suggest you do, then Google will know that you have written all these articles on vitamin D, and see you as more of an authority.

When you think about it in these terms, can you understand why I say abandon automated link builders? The links coming into your pages need to be of the utmost quality and professionalism. They need to build your authority, not ruin it by having some computer-generated article with your name on it linking back to your site.

So, with the idea of quality firmly planted in your mind, let me suggest a few places you could get content published that might actually build your reputation and authority. Before I do that though, I would like to give two general guidelines for backlinking.

1. Only look to get links on authority sites in your niche.
2. Try to be EVERYWHERE.

It doesn't matter if your link is on a Page Rank zero page, as long as that page resides on a site that has good authority. Two of the only measures we have of authority are domain age and domain Page Rank, so I suggest you use these. Look for domains that are 5+ years old, with domain Page Rank of 4 or more and you should be safe.

Anchor text?

With Google Penguin, things have changes a lot.

It used to be the case that to optimize a webpage we'd include our main keyword in the page title, URL, H1 header and several times in the content. We'd then point a lot of backlinks to the page using the main keyword phrase as the anchor text.

Google used to reward this type of optimization.

Then came the Penguin, and as we've seen, that type of optimization is more likely to get your page/site penalized.

As well as de-optimizing on-page factors, we have had to de-optimize backlinks to our pages. In fact, if you check out the Google Webmaster Guidelines, you'll see this as an example of a "link scheme":

Links with optimized anchor text in articles or press releases distributed on other sites. For example:
There are many wedding rings on the market. If you want to have a wedding, you will have to pick the best ring. You will also need to buy flowers and a wedding dress.

Google are clearly cracking down on keyword-rich anchor texts in other documents that point to our site. This type of backlinking used to be the norm, but when we look at those links; they really do look spammy, don't they?

Today we need to be smarter about our backlinks. If we want to survive Google Penguin (and all future algorithm updates), then we cannot create backlinks like this. These are the typical types of backlinks created by automated software tools, so that's another compelling reason not to use software to generate backlinks.

I don't believe that Google will penalize all sites that have **some** backlinks like this. I do, however, believe they will penalize sites where the majority of backlinks are like this, and have probably already done so. What I also think is that the number, or percentage of this type of link, that are "safe", and can occur before a penalty results, is decreasing. Over time, Google are becoming less tolerant (and with the disavow tool, they can do this with a clear conscience). Some data suggests that when Penguin was first released, Google did not penalize sites even when 90% of incoming links were spammy. That percentage has decreased so that today, Google probably penalize sites that have 50% or more spammy incoming links. In the months and years to come, there is no reason to believe that Google won't become even more intolerant. How low will this percentage go? That's anybody's guess, but I have personally stopped all keyword-focused anchor text links to my own sites.

Do you have a site where you've done this in the past? Then you need to be careful and try to water this type of link down by getting better, higher authority backlinks. Remove any poor links that you can, and disavow those that you cannot control.

So what is a safe level for this type of keyword-rich anchor text?

Well, I don't believe there is a safe level. It is certainly a moving target. I know you are probably worrying about your inbound anchor text now, so let me go over what I think would be fairly safe limits. We can then look at what I'd suggest going forward with your backlinking.

I would recommend a link profile to pages on your site where:

1. NO MORE than 5% of backlinks use "topical" anchor text. In fact, I'd recommend you no longer use keywords in anchor text from now on.
2. The other 95% of anchor text should be made up of things like the page URL, the page title, the opening H1 header text, and words that are irrelevant to the topic of the article, like "click here", "read this", "read more", "this site", "this blog", "here", etc. The most natural anchor texts to use for any link to a page on your site are the page title or URL. Those are the ones I recommend you use the most. To help build up keyword anchor text links, consider internal site linking, because that is where **keyword-rich anchor text links become natural**.

OK, let's consider that first point. No more than 5% of backlinks using topical anchor text.

"Topical" anchor text links simply means that the anchor text is related to the topic of your article.

E.g. if your article was on "Potential problems during the last trimester of pregnancy", then topical anchor text links would be stuff like:

• High blood pressure in pregnancy

• Gestational diabetes

• Pre-eclampsia

• Excessive bleeding during pregnancy

• Heartburn in pregnancy

• Groin pain in pregnancy

• Backache during pregnancy

• Pregnancy complications

• Complications in pregnancy

• And so on....

This type of link coming in from another website is considered part of a "link scheme" by Google, and will get you into trouble if you have a lot of links like this.

However, this type of topical anchor text is more natural when one page on your site links to another page on the same site (internal site linking), because it clearly helps your visitors find their way around your site. For links you build to your site, I do not recommend using any more keyword rich anchor text. Save that for internal site linking, and link from other sites using the page title or URL of the page you are linking to.

Ranking for a main keyword phrase?

The old way we did SEO was to find out what people searched for, and then optimize pages around those phrases. That way we could rank higher for the phrases people search for, and get traffic to our website. To a large extent, Hummingbird has changed this, though the changes were apparent long before Hummingbird was released. You can see this if you do a Google search. A lot of the pages that rank for any given term do not contain that term in the title. Some don't even include it on the page.

For example, if I search Google for the term **honey bees dying**, only 2 of the top 10 pages include that exact phrase in the title. Most don't even include that phrase in the web page. The reason these pages are ranked highly is not because of the keyword phrases on the page, it because those pages are themed around the topic of "honey bees dying", so include the words and phrases that Google know should be on those pages. For more details on writing content that is themed around a particular topic, go back and read chapter 1.

Backlinking from now on?

I'm sure you are concerned about building incoming links to your pages. What is the best way to proceed?

Well, the good thing is, Google seem to be paying less attention to inbound anchor text and more attention to the topic of the page linking to yours.

For example, if your page is on "Health benefits of curcumin" and you got a link from a page about curcumin or turmeric, then that link would be a valuable one, irrespective of the anchor text used to link to your page.

With that in mind, I'd suggest trying to make your links look as authoritative as possible. Think how academic literature links to another article. They'll use the title of the other article or the bare URL. They might also use the journal name and edition to help find the document. If you were writing a guest post for another website with the intention of linking back to your site, instead of doing this:

> Curcumin has shown remarkable anti-cancer properties not only in stripping the cancer cells defenses to make them more visible to the body's natural immune system, but also in cell apoptosis.

.. where **anti-cancer properties** is one of the phrases you want to rank for and links to your site. Do something like this instead:

> Curcumin has shown remarkable anti-cancer properties not only in stripping the cancer cells defenses to make them more visible to the body's natural immune system, but in an article "Curcumin initiates cancer cells death", the author describes experimental results showing cell apoptosis occurring.

Do you see how much more this looks like a recommendation to read more information on that topic? Now it looks like something to help the visitor rather than just something used to score points from a search engine? This type of link looks more authoritative, more natural to Google, AND it will be extremely valuable to your site.

If you are submitting articles to other sites for backlinking, then I'd recommend:

1. In-context links like the one above, where the link uses the article title (or URL) and the reader is in no doubt what the destination page is about.
2. A link to a URL or homepage in a resource box, though again, don't use keyword phrases as the anchor text. Use the URL, the domain name or the title of the page you are linking to.

With Penguin, we actually need fewer backlinks to rank well than before, but they need to be from relevant web pages. This isn't just because so many of our competitors were penalized. Google is giving MORE weight to quality links than it used to.

One thing I suggest you do is go after quality links, and then **increase their power** which we'll look at later in the "backlinking the backlinks" section.

OK, where to look for backlinks?

The Best Backlinks

The very best backlinks you can get to your site are the ones you do not create. These are backlinks from other sites, where you did not request the link, nor do you have any say in the anchor text that is used in the link.

These types of backlink are the Holy Grail of backlinks.

They are also the most difficult to get.

The best way of getting this type of link is to develop content that your visitors love, and want to share with others (via their social media channels). Develop content on your site that other site owners will want to link to.

Here are a few ideas:

1. Infographics – these are graphical representations of complex topics. They are very popular items to share on social channels e.g. Pinterest. They are also often re-posted on other sites. When you create and post an infographic on your site, you can include instructions to other webmasters telling them how they can post your infographic on their site (including a link back to your site). You can even include copy & paste code to make things super easy:

2. Scripts & tools that people will bookmark and share. Other webmaster will also link to these. Here is one example of a tool that searches for nutritional information on a food you want to search for:

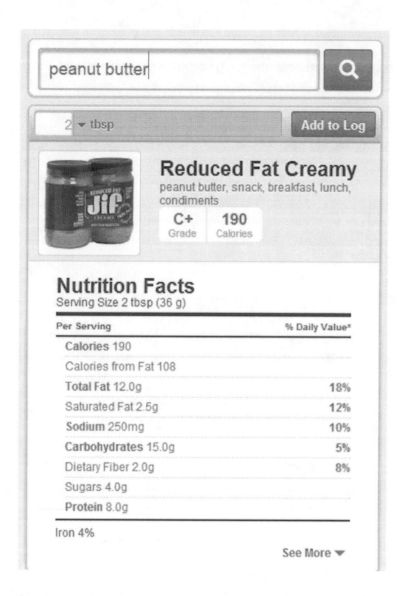

Another good example is a currency convertor script, where you can convert one currency to another. Or a time zone convertor. Any tool that you can create, or get created for your site, that people find useful, will attract links from other websites as well as through social sharing.

3. Forums and places people can come to interact with other people in your niche. For example, if you had a website on "Husky dogs", then a forum would attract Husky owners, who would then recommend your site to their friends and through their social channels. Building user participation on your site is a great way to attract natural links, because anyone interacting on your site becomes a potential link builder for you, when they are on other sites or talking to friends.

4. Free downloads like software or PDFs that people find useful. If you can give these away, and people really do find them useful, your URL will be shared with their friends, on forums they frequent and through their social media channels.

44

5. Posts that include "lists" are the types of posts people love to share on other websites, like forums, in comments on other blogs and via their social channels. For example, "Top 10 Wordpress Plugins" on a site about building websites would be very interesting to people interested in building Wordpress sites. A post like this would get a lot of social shares, plus other sites will link to it. A tip here is to contact the authors of the plugins you recommend, and tell them that they made your top 10 list. Many will link to your post from their site, to prove to their visitors how useful their plugin is.

Use your imagination, and come up with ideas to attract links to your content. These are the most powerful and natural links a site can get, and prove your site's worth to the search engines.

Other backlink sources

This section of the book lists the typical backlink sources recommended by most SEO courses and books. Use these with caution, and I really do recommend you ignore the advice from many SEOs to use keyword rich anchor text.

Article marketing

This is a strange one because some experts believe that article marketing no longer works. I personally believe that it does still work, but, and it's a big but.... don't submit the same article to lots of article directories. A far more productive approach is to pick maybe 10 quality directories and submit a unique article to each one. OK, I hear what you are saying. This means you have to write 10 unique articles. Yes, it does, but if you want to be completely "white hat" about this, and build your authority in a way Google cannot object to, then that is what you need to do. With Google's Panda and now Penguin, this really is the only safe way of doing article marketing. Oh, and don't create backlinks to your own site from within the body of the article. Remember Google's webmaster guidelines?

> * Links with optimized anchor text in articles or press releases distributed on other sites.
>   For example:
>   *There are many wedding rings on the market. If you want to have a wedding, you will have to pick the best ring. You will also need to buy flowers and a wedding dress.*

Forum participation

To a lot of Webmasters, the idea of forums is simply to get backlinks from forum profiles. This is something I DO NOT recommend because it easily detected by Google, as is any page that has a backlink to your site with very little content.

Spammers often use software to automatically create hundreds or thousands of profiles on various forums, including a link back to their site in these profiles. This will get your site into trouble. To me it seems obvious that Google can spot this type of linking very easily. Imagine a website with 5000 forum profile backlinks in a matter of days!

When it comes to forums, the best bang for your buck, so to speak, is to get involved in the forum and help people. Make sure you have a Gravatar image (preferably your photo) attached to the e-mail address of your website, and then the same photo on your website. People will see your posts on lots of forums in your niche. You will start appearing wherever they go, and they are then likely to trust you more and click through to your own website. On your website they will see your picture again and this further reinforces your perceived authority. The more they see your photo and read your contributions on these forums, the more they will recognize and respect you as an authority. This is a great way to build authority and it's nothing to do with the backlinks you can get from the forums, though these are useful as well.

Imagine how much of an authority you will be seen as if a visitor goes to several sites (in your niche) and sees you on all of them, answering questions and providing valuable information.

YouTube & other video sites

Creating videos that offer valuable information in your niche is a great way to increase authority and "social proof" (especially if your photo or brand image appears in the video). Videos that you create do not need to be 10 or 15 minute long, you can easily create short two or three minute videos discussing short issues in your niche. Video descriptions can be quite long, and can **include a link back to your site**. If there is a relevant internal page on your site that makes the most sense to link to, do that, otherwise just link to your homepage.

Sites like YouTube give you your own channel which lists all of your videos. Your YouTube profile can even have a link back to your site, and other sites that are part of your network (Twitter, Facebook, etc). If someone sees one video you have done, and they like it, they can then go and check your channel and see other videos that you've created. From here, they can easily sign up for your Tweets or subscribe to your Facebook page too.

There are a lot of other video sharing sites as well, which will also allow you to have a profile page. Try to use the same photo that you have on your site, and that you are using for your Gravatar. We are trying to build up the recognition factor here so that people can automatically recognize you and think "Oh yes I remember him from..."

Twitter

Again we can use twitter to include a brand photo and link back to our main site. As we add tweets, your photo is sent through the system and ends up again in front of people that have subscribed to your twitter feed. Even if you don't have a lot of followers, your twitter page will have links back to your main site, which adds further authority to your persona.

There are a number of WordPress plugins available which automatically send a tweet for each new post published on your site. I wouldn't rely totally on this plug-in for Twitter "content", as it's important to tweet interesting information you find on a day-to-day basis.

Facebook page

Another way that you can increase your authority is by setting up a Facebook page for your site or your business.

Again there are WordPress plugins that can automatically post to your Facebook page whenever you add new content to your site.

Web 2.0 "Blogs"

There are a number of websites that allow you to set up blogs on their domain. Examples include WordPress.com, Blogger.com (owned by Google), Tumblr.com, and LiveJournal etc. You simply go to the site, sign up, and begin posting to your new blog.

As you add more and more content to these blogs, they become more and more powerful (especially if you build backlinks to these blogs).

Since you add the blog content yourself, you can insert links back to your website, but don't overdo it. These blogs should add value and be high quality, just like every other type of backlink we are looking to build. Set up these blogs and post unique information to each of them. That is how I use them. Create small blogs related to your money site, and add in a link to your money site in a small proportion of the posts you make there. Just make sure the information on these "free blogs" is top quality.

RSS feeds

If you use WordPress to build your site, then you have a feed that contains all of the most recent posts (you define how many posts show in the feed within the WordPress Dashboard). You can find the feed by adding "/feed" to the end of your URL (without the quotes obviously).

For example:

http://ezseonews.com/feed/

Once you have your feed URL, you can submit that feed to a number of different RSS Feed websites.

Every time you add new content to your site, the feed is updated, and you get a link back to the new content.

I don't believe that this type of link helps too much with ranking of pages, especially as posts will slide off the bottom of the feed eventually, but it does help to get new content indexed quickly.

I would recommend submitting your feed to only two or three of the highest authority RSS directories that you can find.

I'd also recommend that you set up your feed to only display excerpts (and a maximum of 10 posts). This should keep you safe from spammers who will try to steal your content by stripping the posts from your feed. Having only 10 posts in the feed is more of a safety precaution as we don't want the last 100 posts hyperlinked on 3 different RSS feed directory sites. This would look a bit too much like we're only doing it to help rankings.

Site directories

Getting your site listed in directories is one of the oldest forms of backlinks. These days, directory listings are not as powerful as they used to be and there are a number of directories you absolutely should not submit your site to.

There are software programs that can submit your site to multiple directories, but I would suggest you save your money and just handpick the most relevant ones (particularly the specialist niche directories that match your chosen niche), and then submit by hand. More is NOT better. Always look for fewer quality submissions where the submission site is a close match to your own. For example, if you have a Paleo diet site, look for directories that specialise in nutrition.

Guest blogging

Guest Blogging is a powerful way to get high quality links back to your site. It's kind of like *Article Marketing 2.0* where you submit articles to sites that accept "guest posts".

The big difference between guest posting and article directories is that guest blogs can be higher quality and much more related to your own niche. For example, you could find a lot of health-related blogs that would accept health related articles from you, but it would be harder to find article directories that were specifically health related.

It works like this:

There are sites out there that are looking for people to write content for them. You write a piece of content and submit it to these sites. If they like your article, they will post it on their website.

When you post your article, you include a resource box that can include links back to your website (or a link in the body of your article). You do need to check the terms and conditions of the sites you are writing for to see whether it's possible to include links within the body of the article. If you can, do that, but make your links look authoritative, like we discussed earlier. Remember, this:

Curcumin has shown remarkable anti-cancer properties not only in stripping the cancer cells defenses to make them more visible to the body's natural immune system, but also in cell apoptosis.

Looks a lot more spammy than this:

Curcumin has shown remarkable anti-cancer properties not only in stripping the cancer cells defenses to make them more visible to the body's natural immune system, but in an article "Curcumin initiates cancer cells death", the author describes experimental results showing cell apoptosis occurring.

The second one is also more Google friendly, as it is not using keyword anchor text. Instead it uses the title of the article being linked to, like a real reference.

Finding Guest Blogs

You can easily find sites that will accept your work by doing a Google search for:

"write for us" + KEYWORD

Where KEYWORD is your main niche word or phrase.

e.g. "write for us" + health

This will return all of the websites that have the phrase "Write for Us" and are related to the health industry. Here are the top few Google results for that term:

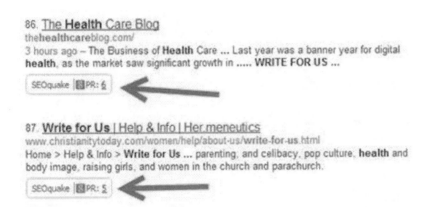

NOTE: PageRank data is being displayed in the SERPs using a free plugin for Firefox, called SEO Quake.

With guest blogging, you can pretty much guarantee getting your content onto high PR websites.

These sites can have a lot of authority in the eyes of Google and are therefore excellent places to get your content published. However, there are other benefits too.

Not only do you get backlinks from an authority site, but you'll also get to post your picture and site URL, which only further boosts your own personal authority in the niche. Each article that gets accepted is exposed to a new audience – one that your own site probably never gets. In this way, guest blogging is a great method to "piggy back" on other peoples traffic.

PDF distribution

PDF files (that can contain links to your website) can be distributed to a number of websites. Again, each site you distribute the PDF to can include your profile picture and link back to your site. To create PDFs, you can use existing content or simply write new content for the PDF file.

Microsoft Word or the free OpenOffice suite, both have built in features to convert text documents into PDF format.

One of the best-known examples of a site that you can upload PDF documents to is:

http://www.scribd.com/

You can find a lot of places to submit PDF documents to by searching Google for "submit ebooks".

Again, like everything else, look for quality sites and think less about quantity.

Important: It is important that the backlink profile to your site is diverse! This means lots of different types of backlinks from a wide range of IP addresses.

When to stop backlinking

If you have the link-bait style content we discussed at the beginning of this section, then your pages will attract links naturally, and you should concentrate on adding new, high quality content to keep your visitors happy and attract new links.

If, however, you don't have content that naturally attracts links, you will be doing some backlinking, and I'd recommend you do so on a continuous basis.

As discussed earlier, I'd recommend using the title of the page you are linking to, or its bare URL as the link text.

Avoid using keyword rich anchor text, because there is a real danger of over-optimization as well as Google simply deciding you have too many spammy links and deciding to penalise your site. If you want keyword rich anchor texts pointing to a page on your site, link to it from other pages on your site.

Now, you may ask how you can get to the top 3 for a phrase if you don't build links with keyword rich anchor text. Well, we are back to a point I made earlier. Does your page deserve to be #1? If it does, then by building overall authority to the site and that page in particular, your page will rise to the top, so there is no need to take risks with more anchor text links. Google knows what your page is about. They don't need over-optimized anchor text to tell them. If they think it's worthy of #1, they'll rank it #1. If they don't, then work more on the quality/value of the content, and authority of your site/page. Also bear in mind Google's Hummingbird algorithm update. Pages that are optimized for a keyword phrase (especially commercial keyword phrases) rarely rank well for that phrase.

Backlinks to backlinks

Whenever you build a site you should be tracking a lot of information. One of the most important things to track is the backlinks pointing to your site.

Majestic SEO is a good free tool to do just this.

Once you have set up Majestic SEO, wait for the data to start coming in.

You will get a list of all the backlinks pointing to your site. Download the list (Majestic allow you to download the list as a spreadsheet) and check them to make sure that the backlinks still exist. Delete any links that no longer exist so you only end up with a list of web pages that actively link to your site.

Now, work your way through the list, and point links to each of these backlinks. You can use any method of backlinking you want but I would recommend you only point quality links at these backlinks. This obviously means more work on your behalf, but I'll explain why it's important a little later. The idea is to make each page linking to one of your pages stronger, and therefore able to pass more link juice to your site.

Here it is as a diagram:

In my opinion, many webmasters go wrong with this type of backlinks to backlinks. They often tend not worry about the quality of the backlinks to their backlinks. Instead they blast thousands of profile links, social bookmarks, spun articles, etc at their main backlinks in an attempt to boost them.

Most webmasters that use this strategy assume that their site is safe, since these poor quality spammy links DO NOT point at their own site, but at the backlinks to their site (these sites that hold our backlinks are often referred to as buffer sites). They assume that these buffer sites provide a type of immunity against a penalty.

However….. Google hates linking schemes, and pyramid systems like this are no exception. Is it too farfetched to think that the negative SEO we saw earlier could render this type of link pyramid not only useless, but harmful to your site? In the diagram above, if those links to your backlinks are good quality, you have nothing to worry about. However, what if those links pointing at your backlinks are low quality, spammy links? Let's re-draw that diagram.

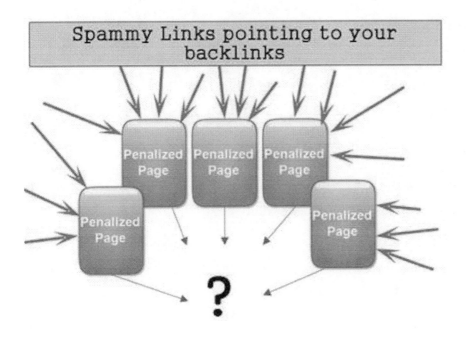

Now, instead of quality links pointing at the backlinks we have poor quality, spammy links, which in turn, penalize the pages that hold your backlinks. What happens now when those pages link to your site?

Page gets a penalty and loses rankings

The penalty would be passed down the pyramid, and your pages are penalized. The idea of being immune to a penalty when linking like this disappeared when Google decided to allow links to pass a negative ranking factor.

Could this happen?

A few years ago, everyone assumed that negative SEO was impossible. That is, if you wanted to take out your competition by pointing a lot of poor links at their site, it wouldn't work. Google even told us it wouldn't work. However, with Penguin (and Panda) we know this is no longer true. The truth is, poor quality inbound links can hurt a webpage.

It makes sense though, doesn't it? I mean *if* Google introduced a system where poor links pass on a negative ranking factor, then they would be wasting a massive opportunity to wipe out a lot of spammers if they didn't allow these penalties to trickle down the link pyramids.

So how do we stop someone else building spammy links to our website in an attempt to take out the competition? Well the simple answer is that we cannot. However Google have given us a tool that we can use to fight back.

The Disavow Tool - How to Fix Bad Links to your Site

Several years ago, webmasters were not held responsible for the links pointing to their own sites. Negative SEO just did not work, and Google themselves told us that bad links could not hurt a site's rankings.

In the last year or two, things changed. Google changed the rules so that bad backlinks could hurt page (and site) rankings. However, because of the whole negative SEO angle, Google needed to provide a system where webmasters truly could be held accountable for the links to their sites, whether they had created them or not. In other words, if a website became the target of a negative SEO campaign, Google wanted the webmaster to have the power to fix it. The Disavow tool was born.

The Disavow tool allows webmasters to report bad links pointing at their sites, in the hope that Google will not count them as part of that site's backlink profile.

Therefore, if someone points a lot of spammy links at your site to try to get your site penalized, you now have a tool that you can use to tell Google about those links, and hopefully get them devalued to the point where they don't contribute to your rankings.

Before we look at the Disavow tool, let me just state something. Just because we can report bad links to Google, does not mean Google will listen or take action. Google have said that webmaster should use the Disavow tool as a last resort. The first step should always be to contact webmasters who are linking to you and ask for links to be removed. If those

56

webmasters refuse to remove links, or ignore your requests, then that is what the Disavow tool is for.

Checking your Link Profile & Creating a Disavow File

The first step in using the Disavow tool is to find the links that point to your site and evaluate them. You need to identify the links that may be causing your site harm. These links include:

1. Those on pages with scraped content.
2. Links on pages with spun content.
3. Links on pages with very poor/limited content (in terms of language, spelling, grammar, etc).
4. Links on sites that have been penalised in Google.
5. Links on irrelevant sites, or sites with dubious content.
6. Site-wide links that appear on all of the pages of a linking website.
7. Any link that you would not want Google to manually inspect.

Fortunately, Google Webmaster Tools provides us with an easy way to do a link audit. Of course, you need a Webmaster Tools account for this, with your site linked to that account.

Assuming you have had your website linked to your Webmaster Tools account for a while, Google will list the backlinks to your site.

To find these, log in to Webmaster Tools and click on the site you want to inspect.

Now in the menu on the left, select **Links to You Site** from the **Search Traffic** menu.

On the right, you'll see a list of links to your site:

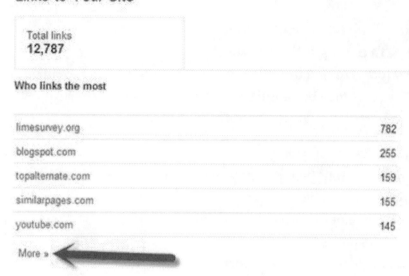

Google only show you a few by default, but if you look at the bottom of the list, you'll see a link to **More**.

Click it.

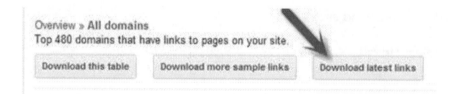

You now have a button to **Download latest links**. Clicking this button will allow you to choose the format of the download.

The CSV format will download a spreadsheet you can view in Excel or similar spreadsheet program. Alternatively, you can download in Google Docs format.

If you don't use Google Docs, I recommend you give it a try. Just go to **docs.google.com**

Login to Google Docs with your Gmail address and password.

If you select Google Docs from Webmaster Tools and click the OK button, the spreadsheet opens directly in Google Docs:

This spreadsheet lists all links Google want you to know that point to your site.

Not only do you get the URL, you also get the date that the link was first discovered. This means you can check all of the links the very first time you do a link audit, and then in a month or two, you only need to check the new links that Google are reporting since your last check.

You need to work your way through the list of links, and pull out any that you really think are harming your website.

Google give you two ways to deal with bad links. You can either report them on a link by link basis, or you can report a whole domain so any links on that domain will be disavowed. You can create a plain text file to use as your disavow list.

To disavow a single URL, just list the URLs, one on each line.

The format for reporting an entire domain is as follows:

Domain:somebaddomain.com

Google also encourage you to use comments in your disavow file. These comments can be for you, or for Google, outlining steps you have carried out to get links removed. For example, if you have tried contacting a webmaster linking to your site, and they have ignored your requests, you can include the comment in your disavow file, before listing the appropriate URLs or domain.

Comments are included by simply using the # symbol. A valid comment would be something like this:

Webmaster has ignored my request to remove these links

If you want to write more, just go onto a second line, with the # at the start. For example:

Webmaster has not replied to my emails requesting link removal

Contacted on 16/08/2013 and again on 06/09/2013

Google provide the following example as a valid disavow file:

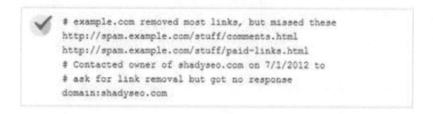

```
# example.com removed most links, but missed these
http://spam.example.com/stuff/comments.html
http://spam.example.com/stuff/paid-links.html
# Contacted owner of shadyseo.com on 7/1/2012 to
# ask for link removal but got no response
domain:shadyseo.com
```

In their example, they want two URLs disavowed, plus all links on the shadyseo.com domain.

One you have built up your disavow file, you need to upload it to Google. One thing I recommend you do is to add the following comment to the beginning of your disavow file:

Last updated 10/10/2013

Save the file to your hard disk, so next time you want to do a link audit, you know the date of your last audit and can just look at the new links since that date (remember that Google give us the date a link was found).

Uploading the disavow file to Google is simple.

Go to this URL:

https://www.google.com/webmasters/tools/disavow-links-main

You will need to login using your Webmaster Tools login details (if you are not already logged in).

Select the website from the drop down list, and click the Disavow button:

Webmaster Tools

You will get a warning before you can upload the file you created earlier:

Disavow Links

This is an advanced feature and should only be used with caution. If used incorrectly, this feature can potentially harm your site's performance in Google's search results. We recommend that you only disavow backlinks if you believe that there are a considerable number of spammy, artificial, or low-quality links pointing to your site, and if you are confident that the links are causing issues for you.

Disavow Links

If you want to proceed, click the **Disavow Links** button.

61

Disavow Links

This is an advanced feature and should only be used with caution. If us potentially harm your site's performance in Google's search results. W disavow backlinks if you believe that there are a considerable number c quality links pointing to your site, and if you are confident that the links

Upload a text file (*.txt) containing **only** the links you want to disavow.

Now you have a button to **Choose File**. Click that and select your disavow text file.

Finally, click the **Submit** button to upload the file to Google.

Updating the Disavow file

When you need to update the disavow file (e.g. to include more URLs or domains), simply add the new URLs and domains to the file, change the comment at the top to the current date so you can keep track, then come back to the disavow tool and re-upload your updated file. Google only keep one file per site, so the last one you upload will be the file they use for any "disavowing".

I'd recommend you do a complete link audit on your site, and then check new links every month or two. Now that you are responsible for all links to your site, you need to know who is linking to your site, and whether those links are potentially harmful to your rankings. If they are, disavow them.

I also want you to think about something else.

If there is a spammy web page linking to you, and you know that it can only be harmful to your rankings, it is possible that the site in question has more than one link to your site, even though you are not aware of them all. In cases like this, I always disavow the whole site rather than just the URLs. If the page on that site is so bad you want to disavow it, then chances are that the whole site is pretty bad.

Summary of Backlinks

I have listed some of my favorite sources of backlinks, though the list is certainly not definitive. There are things like blog commenting and social bookmarking that a lot of people recommend. I wouldn't overdo either of these sources though (or in fact any one source), and always maintain the Quality rule in every backlink you get.

Just remember these simple guidelines. When getting links:

1. Try to get links from as many different places as possible (we want IP diversity).
2. Look for quality rather than quantity. A handful of quality links will do more for your rankings than hundreds or thousands of spammy links (which actually could get your site penalized).
3. Vary your link text. If you have an article on "Flax seeds", check out the Google keyword tool to see what people are searching for when trying to find information on flax seeds. Use these **search phrases** in your link text as well as your **domain name**, **domain URL**, **the title of the page you are linking to** and even phrases like "**click here**", or "**this article**", just to get variation (which seems very important with Google Penguin). I don't recommend you use any one anchor text more than 5% of the time, and instead, **rely on your themed content to tell Google what the page should rank for**. In total, your "optimized links" should not be more than about 30% of all links pointing to a page.
4. Backlink your backlinks to make them stronger, but only backlink using high quality links. By strengthening your backlinks like this, you'll need fewer of them to compete.
5. Carry out a link audit periodically on your site, and disavow any low quality, spammy links that may be affecting your rankings.

4. What's in it for the visitor?

When somebody arrives on your website, you have a very short time to make a first impression. That first impression will decide whether they stay or go, so the first thing you need to do is make sure your site looks good. If you're using WordPress, then that's quite easy because there are a lot of very attractive WordPress designs out there.

Apart from the design, another aspect of your site which will add to that first impression is the speed at which the page loads. This needs to be as fast as possible to avoid having visitors waiting for stuff to load.

Install Google Analytics and get a Google Webmaster Tools account

These tools can give you a huge amount of information on your site and your visitors. They are also Google's way to communicate with YOU! If there is anything Google in concerned about, they'll tell you about it in your Webmaster account. They'll also notify you when your site is down or there is a WordPress upgrade (if you use WordPress).

A lot of webmasters think it's best to avoid these tools as Google will use them against you, but I disagree. Google already has all the data they need on your site, Google Tools are their way of sharing that data with you.

Google's "Webmaster Tools" use to tell you how fast your site was loading and show you a graph of load times over a period of time. However, they have since retired this tool. You can now find that information in Google Analytics though.

A great alternative to checking your site load times is to use an online tool like GTMetrix. You simply enter your page URL and GTMetrix will measure the load speed there and then, in real-time:

Not only do they give you time in seconds for the page load, but they'll tell you which parts of your site are slowing the load time down, and what you can do to fix the problems.

Website stickiness

In Google Analytics, Google will tell you the average time a visitor stays on your site, as well as the bounce rate (how quickly someone bounces back to Google after reaching your site).

Bounce rate and time on site are a measure of how "Sticky" your site is.

Here is the bounce rate for one of my sites over the last month:

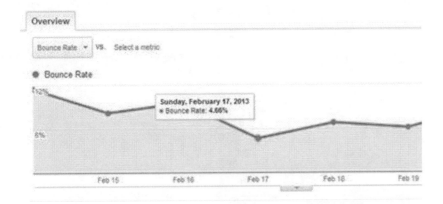

You'll notice that the maximum bounce rate over the last month was around 30%, with the average less than half that. This means that only around 15% of people visiting my site go straight back to Google after reaching the landing page. Here are the averages for this site over the last month:

Avg. Visit Duration: 00:16:32

Bounce Rate: 14.71%

% New Visits: 80.61%

Average bounce rate of 14.7% and average time on site of over 16 minutes. I'd say that the site was quite sticky, wouldn't you?

You can examine these metrics for individual pages to see where your site is being let down by any content that does not hold the visitors attention.

The next screenshot shows the data for a number of URLs on my site.

Avg. Visit Duration	% New Visits	Bounce Rate
00:17:10	54.50%	7.75%
01:58:04	42.35%	0.00%
00:27:08	83.72%	9.30%
00:15:53	94.59%	18.92%
00:14:28	79.31%	24.14%
00:06:05	85.19%	11.11%
00:06:47	92.31%	19.23%
00:07:52	92.00%	4.00%
00:05:26	100.00%	29.17%
00:10:51	73.91%	8.70%

Just look for the pages with the lowest "visit duration" and the highest "bounce rate" and see if there is something you can do about them to improve the overall experience on your site. Any page with a high bounce rate is a clear indicator that it is not giving the visitor the "experience" they are looking for.

Important aspects of a web page

You need to capture the visitor's attention and let them know what you have got for them.

In terms of articles on your website, this can mean an eye catching headline that makes them want to read more. If your visitor reads the headline and finds it interesting, they'll then read the first paragraph. The first paragraph is almost as vital as the headline itself, so you might like to try creating an opening paragraph as a summary of what your visitor will find further down the page.

As you write content, try to keep sentences short (20 – 25 words) as well as paragraphs – four or five sentences. People hate large blocks of text, but also hate sentences that are so long they become confusing. When you have finished your content, read it aloud and make sure there are no parts that you have to reread to understand fully, and no parts that you hesitate over as you read them.

To make your article easier to read, use sub-heading and bullet points. Pictures and diagrams can also help break up blocks of text, making it easier for the visitor. It's like that old adage goes; a picture is worth a thousand words.

NOTE: Use ALT tags on images, but do not keyword stuff them. Simply use an ALT tag that describes the image.

Another important point is to use colors and fonts wisely. Don't put white fonts on black background or any other combination that causes eye strain. Black font on white backgrounds is the best, and use fonts that are designed to work online like the Verdana, Trebuchet and Georgia. If you want to see some truly shocking use of colors on the web, search Google images for the term **bad website design**.

While we're talking about content, be aware that people are a lot less patient than they used to be, so be succinct and to the point. Don't waffle just to get the number of words on the page higher.

To make your site sticky, you need to give your visitors what they want. In order to do that you need to know your visitor. Ask yourself:

• Who is it?

• What do they want?

• What answers to they need?

• What do they want to ask me?

If we are talking about your homepage, this should guide them quickly and easily to the various sections of your website that gives them what they want. Your visitor should be able to find what they require swiftly and effortlessly. Needless to say a search box is essential, but that is easy with WordPress ;)

Ways to build Trust

1. A photo of yourself in a prominent position on your website. The sidebars or in the logo are a good place for this. A photo helps build trust because the visitor can see who they are interacting with. The problem for Internet Marketers is that not many want their photos on their niche websites. I would suggest though that the benefits of having a photo are too strong to ignore.

2. If you use your photo as a Gravatar, then every time you post comments on other sites, your photo will appear. This goes back to what we were saying in the section on building authority. How much more comforting is it for a visitor to arrive on your site and see a face they've seen

67

before on other authority sites? This can really help towards building a high level of trust.

3. Fresh content - If people arrive at your site and see that the content is several years old, this may be enough for them to click the back button. Keep stuff like reviews up to date. If you update a review, change the timestamp of the post in WordPress to reflect the new date. If the content is "ageless", remove the date/time stamp from the post (some knowledge of PHP or WordPress templates is required for this).

4. A clearly visible privacy policy, terms of use and a contact page (and even an About Us page where you can mention who you are and what goals you have for the site), are great ways to help build trust. On your contact page you should ideally have a real address as this helps with the trust building. Again, it's a good idea to have your photo on the contact us page.

Types of content that can give your visitors what they want:

1. Answering real questions – you can find questions that people ask in your niche by looking at Yahoo Answers, Wordtracker's Free Question Tool, Quora and even Ask.com.   Find real questions and provide accurate answers.

2. Buyer guides – e.g. if your site is about Android Tablets, give your visitors a free PDF that tells them what they need to know when it comes to buying one. You can use that free guide to build a list if you want, by making visitors opt-in to your list before they are given the download URL.

   Tutorials – Provide helpful tutorials for your visitors if you can think of some that are relevant to your niche.

3. Videos - Create informative, relevant videos and have them embedded in your web pages. Put a great title above the video to make sure your visitor clicks to watch (never have them start automatically – give your visitor the option). Make sure the video content lives up to the title! Upload videos to Youtube.com and develop your own YouTube channel in your chosen niche. This will not only bring traffic, but also build credibility and trust. You can link to this channel from your site.

4. One type of page I usually include on my niche sites is a Terminology page. A niche has its own vocabulary as we have seen, and often people want to know what certain words or phrases mean. You can see an example of this type of page listing on diabetes terminology.

   The best advice I can give is to ask you a question.

   What valuable information or resources can you offer that are not available on the top 10 pages in Google?

Make your site interactive

1. Allow Comments from visitors at the end of your articles. Invite or encourage your visitors to use the comment box. It's amazing how simple it is to say "Hey, if you've got a question or an opinion on this, leave a comment at the bottom of this post", yet a lot of people don't bother. Darren Rowse wrote a nice article on getting your visitors to comment. A lot of people turn comments off on their blog because of the huge amounts of spam they receive. However, by using a good spam blocker like Akismet (commercial) or Growmap Anti Spambot Plugin, or GASP for short (free), you can eliminate 99% of all spam.
   Comments allow your visitor to interact with YOU (and other commenters) but if they ask a question, make sure you answer it as this starts a dialogue with your target audience and builds trust and authority when visitors see that you're answering their questions personally.
   Answering questions brings visitors back to your site, especially if you have a plug-in installed

that allows them to track responses to their comments. A popular one is "Comment Reply Notification".

2. By using a ratings and review plug-in (search the WordPress plugin directory for one), you can give your visitors the chance to award products their own star rating when they leave a comment.

3. Polls – Allow your visitors to express their opinion by voting. There are free polling scripts available.

4. Provide Social Media Icons after each post so that people can spread the word on your great content. There are a number of free plugins available. Shane Melaugh created a great free one called Social Essentials. It gives you a decent set of options as well as stats on social shares.

5. Add a forum. This can be a lot of work because forums are often spammed heavily, but forums are a great way for people to interact with yourself and others. Several WordPress plugins are available that will add a fully functional forum on your site.

That's it! That's my SEO guide for 2013 and beyond.

So what's next?

For anyone interested in learning my own methods for building authority sites, backlinking and SEO in general, you can join my free internet marketing newsletter.

Finally I want to wish you good luck, and I hope that you enjoyed this book.

Please leave a review on Amazon

If you did (or even if you didn't), PLEASE add a review on the Amazon website. You can find the book listing here:

Amazon US

Amazon UK

You can find this book on other Amazon stores by searching for its ASIN - B0099RKXE8

All the best

Andy Williams

More Information from Dr. Andy Williams

If you would like more information, tips, tutorials or advice, there are two resources you might like to consider.

The first is my free weekly newsletter over at ezSEONews.com offering tips, tutorials and advice to online marketers and webmasters. Just sign up and my newsletter plus SEO articles will be delivered to your inbox. I cannot always promise a weekly schedule, but I try ;)

I also run a course over at CreatingFatContent.com, where I build real websites in front of members in "real-time" using my system of SEO.

An SEO Checklist

A step-by-step plan for fixing SEO problems with your web site

By Dr. Andy Williams

http://ezseonews.com

What people are saying about this book

"This is the most concise but complete guide to useful SEO that I've seen anywhere since the Google updates." **Karl Steppens**

"Dr. Andy really is an authority on SEO and I highly recommend this book to all webmasters." **DebV**

"This book was very informative and easy to follow. Many great reminders and new information I didn't know." **D Eastman**

"This was a good read because it breaks it down into sections and talks to you like an everyday Joe, so that even inexperienced computer users can see the sense in what is being explained to them." **Miss Winters**

"The author was one of the first "gurus" that I followed, and I've found him well-informed, creative, and generous through the years." **Lane P. Lester**

"Extremely useful information for anyone who has a website or is interested in building one. As always, what I particularly like about Andy's books is that he gives great information which is not padded out with loads of waffle. A good, helpful read." **Linda Plummer**

"What I like is that each issue is explained, so I get to understand why I need to do something. And that legitimate practices are described, so I don't have to worry that Google is going to penalize my website....

... Because it is really a checklist, an actionable one and easy to understand, even you are a non techie like I am." **Francesca CH**

"The author, Andy Williams, is one of the few SEO experts that I listen to as he has integrity, seeks to help people, and offers very useful information." **Jack Raburn**

" I've followed Andy's stuff for many years; he's concise, articulate, precise and careful to give only advice that he's tested himself. This book is in line with all his other guides and information - it's no-fluff, no-BS and thoroughly tested to give you the best advice available right now. If you're lost in the SEO maze, do exactly what he says and you won't believe how easy SEO can be!" **Isobel DeSantis**

Why this book?

I've already written an SEO book called SEO 2014 & Beyond (http://www.amazon.com/dp/B0099RKXE8) which is available on Amazon Kindle format, so why this new book?

The original book is an overall strategy for SEO that works. The book is particularly useful for those looking to learn SEO or catch up on recent changes with Google and what that means to the webmaster. However, for many of my students and clients, the biggest problem is where to start on an existing site that has lost its rankings. We've all been there. Everything is going really well, and then you wake up one day to find your Google traffic wiped out. What do you do next?

This book will take you by the hand and guide you through a complete checklist of things you should objectively critique/fix on your website. Now, before I go on, I need to point out that a lot of people are not very objective about their own work. It's often hard to take criticism from other people and even harder to admit that we made a mistake somewhere along the way. However, for this process to work, you need to step outside of yourself and try to view your website as a complete stranger would see it on arrival.

I'd also like to say that although you do need to be critical, I don't want you to be too hard on yourself. Nearly everyone I know lost a site or two in the Google updates of the last 2 years. I lost quite a few myself. The reason why so many people were caught out was the simple fact that Google had moved the goalposts somewhat.

Pre-Panda and pre-Penguin, Google tolerated certain activities. Post-Panda and post-Penguin, they don't. As a result, they are now enforcing their Webmaster Guidelines, something that SEOs never really believed Google would do! It's this change in tolerance that got so many of us into trouble.

Let me give you an example of the moving goal posts.

We have known for some time that Google doesn't like us building backlinks to our site with automated tools. How did we know? Google told us. So why did so many people engage in link-building campaigns using automated tools that created hundreds or thousands of low quality links in a short space of time? The answer is simple. At the time, Google tolerated this behavior and even rewarded it. When you see your competitor building all these links and jumping ahead of you in the search engine results, it's only natural that you want to do the same to get your rankings back, right? I mean Google is rewarding that behavior with better rankings, so it must be OK.

As long as Google openly tolerated this type of link-building, it would continue, and Google knew that.

Google Panda, and probably more specifically Google Penguin, changed all this. Google went from being a very tolerant search engine, to one of zero tolerance and the most recent Penguin update on 22nd May 2013 is the clearest signal of intent from Google.

For as long as I can remember, Google has published Webmaster Guidelines to tell us what they consider acceptable and what is not. Before Panda and Penguin, these were simply that – **guidelines** that we could choose to ignore. With the arrival of Panda and Penguin, these guidelines became **rules**.

All of the "illicit" activities (like link building) that were previously tolerated are now a noose around the neck of the website. Webmasters who may have held the number one spot for years, suddenly found their site gone from page one. Many were even gone from Google altogether.

The reason so many websites lost their rankings was simply because those sites had not followed the guidelines in the past.

I wrote this book to help you more easily identify and fix the problems you may have with your website. It's the same SEO checklist that I use on my student's websites and those of my clients.

How to use this book

I've divided the areas you need to look at into 10 "Checkpoint" chapters. They are:

• Checklist Point #1 – The Domain Name

• Checklist Point #2 – Web Page Real Estate

• Checklist Point #3 – Site Structure

• Checklist Point #4 – Comments

• Checklist Point #5 – Social Presence

• Checklist Point #6 – Would you Trust the site?

• Checklist Point #7 – Bounce Rates & Time on Site

• Checklist Point #8 – Legal pages

• Checklist Point #9 – Content Quality

• Checklist Point #10 – Inbound Link Profiles

These will tell you what you need to be looking out for as well as the theory behind why you need to make these checks. Each Checkpoint chapter ends with a bulleted "checklist" of things you should check in that area.

If you like, you can work your way through the book, checking off each point as you go. However, you might like to read the whole book first and then take action once you understand all of the areas that need your attention.

To make things easier for you, at the end of the book, I've compiled a master checklist that includes all of the checkpoints mentioned throughout the book.

OK, let's start off by looking at what Google actually want.

What does Google want?

Before we start the checklist, I thought it would be a good idea to explain what it is that Google actually wants. You can read their guidelines for yourself, here:

http://bit.ly/tGftAJ

Near the top of that page, it says:

"Even if you choose not to implement any of these suggestions, we strongly encourage you to pay very close attention to the "Quality Guidelines," which outline some of the illicit practices that may lead to a site being removed entirely from the Google index or otherwise impacted by an algorithmic or manual spam action."

It is really important that you take this statement seriously. Google will remove or penalize your site if they catch you carrying out any activities they don't approve of.

To make things worse for anyone trying to fly under the Google radar, they also state:

"If you believe that another site is abusing Google's quality guidelines, please let us know by filing a spam report."

That phrase "spam report" is hyperlinked to an online form!

Google are trying to get other webmasters to report websites that ignore their guidelines and use shady techniques. That means your competitors can report your site if they see you doing something to cheat the system!

But what do Google consider "illicit practices"?

Here is a list of some things you need to avoid.

• **Pages that are designed for the search engines, not for the visitor**. We've all seen these in the search engine results pages (SERPs). They are pages that are designed with the sole purpose of ranking well in Google, without any care to what the visitor might think when they arrive. Google want engaging, unique content (and I'm talking unique in terms of "voice", discussion or ideas, not just the words and their order on the page).

• **Any trick or "loophole" designed to help a PageRank better in the search engine**. That pretty much covers most of SEO as we used to know it!

• **Content that is auto-created using a software tool**. Most software tools throw out gibberish so this is a fairly obvious point. One type of tool that deserves special attention is article

80

spinners (which gained a lot of followers in the last few years). Spinners can produce hundreds of near perfect "unique" articles in just a few minutes in the hands of an expert. These spun articles have been used extensively in backlinking campaigns, by many people, but Google are now on the warpath.

Other examples of auto-generated content include articles translated by software (badly) without a human review, scraped content from RSS feeds and "stitching or combining content from different web pages without adding sufficient value." This last point should be of interest to content curators who don't add value to the content they curate.

• **Any "linking schemes" that are designed to manipulate a web PageRank in the search engine**. Wow. That's a big one. Google have told us there that they don't want us building links to our site for the sole purpose of better rankings! But backlinking is one of the most effective ways to improve your rank in Google, so obviously we all do it. Just linking two or more of your own sites together could be considered a linking scheme if the sole point is to help those sites rank better. Other things Google don't like are sites that buy (or sell) links to pass Page Rank (PR), reciprocal linking between sites, and websites that have used automated tools to build backlinks. Google don't even like links inserted into posts you write for other sites (guest posts), if those links are simply there to manipulate your web page rankings.

• **Websites that serve up one version of a page to the search engines, yet a different page to the visitors**. This is called cloaking and is commonly used by webmasters trying to trick the search engines into ranking the "sales" page higher. The page the search engines see is keyword rich (helping the page to rank), whereas the version the visitors see is completely different. Similar to cloaking is "sneaky redirects". This is often achieved with JavaScript or a Meta refresh so that the page the visitor sees is not the same page that the search engine spider crawled and was ultimately ranked for in Google.

• **Pages that have "hidden" text**. In other words, text that is invisible to the visitor. This is commonly done using CSS to make the text the same color as the background. Visitors don't see the text, yet the search engines do (since they read the text based document).

• **Websites that use "doorway pages"**. These are poor quality pages that are designed to rank for a single keyword. Sites that employ doorway pages often have hundreds or thousands of them, where their sole purpose is to rank high for a single search term and deliver visitors from the search engine. An example is a website that has lots of pages of similar content, with each page trying to rank for a different geographical location by changing the title and main location based phrases.

• **Affiliate websites that don't add enough value**. These include the typical Amazon affiliate website where each page is a review of a product that links to Amazon. The problem occurs when the review content contains nothing that isn't already found on Amazon or the manufacturers own website. Affiliate sites MUST add significant value.

Some things Google actually recommend you do

• **Use clear, intuitive navigation on your site with text links**. Every page on your site needs to be reachable from a link somewhere on the site. A sitemap helps here (and Google recommends you have one), but it is also a good idea to interlink your content if it helps the visitor navigate your site.

• **Don't have too many links on any given page**. Sites like Wikipedia (http://www.wikipedia.org/) seem to ignore this rule yet still rank well for a huge number of searches. However, Wikipedia seems to have been accepted and trusted by Google, so what's good for them may not be good for you.

• **Websites that have useful, information-rich content**. Think here in terms of content written for the visitor, not for the search engine.

• **ALT tags that actually describe the image**. Since ALT tags are often "read" by software for blind visitors, they are very important sources of information for people that cannot actually see the image.

• **Sites should not have broken links**. There is a good free software tool called Xenu Link Sleuth (http://bit.ly/cijL) that can spider your site and check this for you. There really is no excuse.

OK, you get the idea.

We'll look at some of the other things Google like and don't like as we work our way through the checklist, so let's get on with the "SEO Checklist".

The SEO Checklist

Checklist Point #1 – The domain name

Exact Match Domains

In the past, keywords in your domain name helped your website rank better. The ultimate ranking boost was from something called an Exact Match Domain or EMD for short. An EMD took keyword "stuffing" to the extreme – by making the domain name the same as the man keyword phrase you are trying to target.

For example, if you wanted to rank well for "buy prescription drugs online", then the exact match domain would be buyprescriptiondrugsonline.XXX where XXX is any one of the domain TLDs (.com, .net, .org etc). Merely having that exact phrase in the domain name gave you an unfair ranking advantage. SEOs soon spotted this and EMDs became hot favorites for anyone trying to make money online.

On 28th September 2012, Matt Cutts (head of Google's webspam team) tweeted the following:

Matt Cutts ✅
@mattcutts

📣 Follow

Minor weather report: small upcoming Google algo change will reduce low-quality "exact-match" domains in search results.

← Reply   ↻ Retweet   ★ Favorite   ••• More

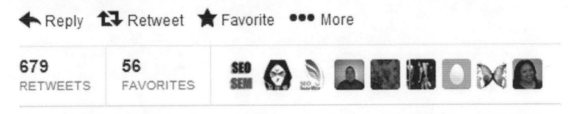

679
RETWEETS

56
FAVORITES

1:43 PM - 28 Sep 12

Google had finally decided to take action on "low-quality" EMDs and prevent them from ranking simply because of the phrase in the domain name.

Now, if you have an EMD, don't panic. Google's algorithm changes were designed to remove **low quality EMDs** from the search results, not good sites that happen to be on an EMD (though

83

there is often some collateral damage with big changes to the algorithm, so some good sites were probably hit too). You need to decide if your site is a quality EMD or a low quality one.

Some things to look for that might indicate a low quality EMD site:

• Is the site specifically targeting that EMD phrase or does your site have a lot of quality content within the overall niche?

• Do you have a lot of backlinks with anchor text that matches the EMD phrase?

• Are there very few pages on your site?

• Reading your content, does there appear to be a bias towards using that EMD phrase (to try to help it rank better)?

• Is that EMD phrase repeated a few times on the homepage? What about other pages on the site?

• Is that phrase used in internal links back to the homepage from other pages on the site?

• Is your on-site SEO targeting that EMD phrase?

• Is the EMD phrase one that AdWords Advertisers are willing to bid on? Is it quite commercial?

As an example, here are the estimated costs per click for some contact lens related phrases (as shown in Google's Keyword Tool (http://bit.ly/MmYK4f):

☐	**contact lenses** online order ▾	€5.96
☐	contacts lenses online ▾	€5.65
☐	buy **contact lenses** on line ▾	€5.60
☐	ordering **contact lenses** online ▾	€5.56
☐	order contacts lenses online ▾	€5.55
☐	order contacts online ▾	€5.52
☐	online contacts lenses ▾	€5.52

Any of those phrases turned into an EMD would be suspect.

Take that first phrase as an example. The EMD would be:

contactlensesonlineorder.com

Surely someone would have registered that in the past to take advantage of EMD ranking power? If they could rank for that phrase and slap AdSense ads on the site, then they'd be making a good chunk of change every time someone clicked on an advert.

Typing that domain into my web browser, this is what I get:

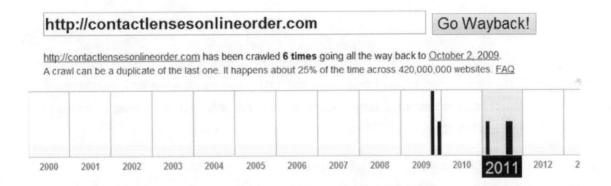

Oops! Google Chrome could not find contactlensesonlineorder.com

Suggestions:
• Search on Google:

contact lenses online order   Google Search

However, if I search the **Way Back Machine** (http://web.archive.org), which looks for archived versions of the website, this is what I see:

http://contactlensesonlineorder.com   Go Wayback!

http://contactlensesonlineorder.com has been crawled **6 times** going all the way back to October 2, 2009.
A crawl can be a duplicate of the last one. It happens about 25% of the time across 420,000,000 websites. FAQ

| 2000 | 2001 | 2002 | 2003 | 2004 | 2005 | 2006 | 2007 | 2008 | 2009 | 2010 | 2011 | 2012 | 2 |

That site existed in 2009, and then again in 2011.

Using Way Back Machine, I can even take a look at that site as it appeared back in 2009 or 2011. Here it is in 2009:

Contact Lenses Online Order

Save up to 70% off retail contact lens prices. Fast, Simple and Cheap.

- Acuvue
- Biomedics
- Freshlook
- Soflens
- Proclear

We carry all popular brands of contact lenses including Acuvue, Biomedics, Focus, Freshlook, Soflens, Order your contact lenses, and save up to 70% off contact lens prices.

Best Seller Contact Lenses

Notice the main header on the page uses the exact same phrase. This is typical of low quality EMDs.

So, why is that EMD no longer an active site?

Perhaps Google's plan to wipe out low quality EMDs worked and it no longer made money, so they let it expire? No-one wants it now because of the problems associated with this type of EMD, and the fact that the domain may have picked up a penalty (which isn't always removed when a domain changes hands).

Using Way Back Machine to find problem domains

If your domain has never ranked properly, then I'd recommend that you check it at the Way Back Machine website. You will then be able to see if your domain was used before you got your hands on it. If it was, what was the site like previously? It is possible that a domain could have been penalized in the past, and that domain penalty carried over to the new owner. If this is the case, you could file a reconsideration request at Google (http://bit.ly/sRDmul). While not guaranteed to work, it might if Google can see the domain has changed hands.

Keyword stuffed domains

Another potential problem with a domain name is keyword stuffing.

Let's suppose your website is selling cosmetic contact lenses. If your domain was **cosmetic-halloween-colored-contact-lenses.com** then it's clear that the domain has been stuffed with relevant keywords. This would get you into trouble, but even if it didn't, what would visitors think to a domain like that? This type of domain is not one that I would be anxious to hold on to.

Back in March 2011, Matt Cutts discussed the use of keywords in the domain name in a YouTube video:

http://bit.ly/gWljCy

He suggests that a brandable domain is probably better than a keyword rich domain (and I agree). Despite being old, that video hints about the changes to come in the way keyword rich domains are ranked.

Of course, these are just general guidelines on domain names. There isn't much you can do about your domain name once you have it. Your choice is to either stick with it or move your site to a different domain. In this video, Matt Cutts offers some advice on moving a domain:

http://bit.ly/pzhGLX

The domain name checklist

• EMD? If yes, then be aware that this will work against you and you'll need to de-optimize the site for the phrase in the domain name.

• Keyword stuffed? There isn't much you can do with this other than move the site to a better domain. Keyword stuffed domains look spammy and don't instill much confidence in visitors. Unless there is good reason to keep the domain (like it still makes good income or ranks well), I'd consider moving the site to a better, more brandable domain.

• Has your domain never ranked properly? If not, then check its history at the Way Back Machine. Consider submitting a reconsideration request at Google if it looks like the domain was used by someone else in the past.

Checklist Point #2 – Web page real estate

Above the fold

In January 2012, Google released a document that outlined a new "page layout algorithm improvement". You can read it here:

http://bit.ly/HSXQHj

In releasing this change, Google were hoping to improve the user experience. No one likes to arrive at a website if all they see in their browser are Google ads, banners or email subscription forms. The general idea of this update was to penalize sites that didn't have much useful content above the fold. "Above the fold" simply means the viewable area in your browser before you scroll down the page.

In the past, a lot of people made a lot of money throwing up "AdSense sites". These were designed to rank well, but show the visitors very little content, just money-generating adverts. Visitors could either click an advert (and make the webmaster money), click the back button on their browser, or scroll down the page to find the content. Because of the poor user experience on these sites, most people probably opted for one of the first two options as they figured the content would not be up to much. If something caught their eye in the adverts, they'd most probably click there.

NOTE: If you are a member of Google AdSense yourself, you will probably have been told by the AdSense team to put MORE adverts on your pages. The Google AdSense team seems to be at odds with what the Google Search Engine actually wants. Be aware that the two parts work separately and want to achieve different things.

Look at your page above the fold. I'd actually recommend resizing your browser to 1024x768 (most people use this resolution or something higher these days according to **W3Schools.com** - http://bit.ly/bGhfb0) and seeing what is above the fold on your site.

Once resized, is there meaningful content? If you removed the adverts from that area, would it still offer value to the visitors in terms of the other content above the fold? This is also an interesting test for your page as a whole. If you remove the adverts from a page, would the remaining content be seen as high quality? It should!

NOTE: If you have some adverts above the fold, you may be OK. On the page layout algorithm announcement, Google say:

> *"This algorithmic change does not affect sites who place ads above-the-fold to a normal degree, but affects sites that go much further to load the top of the page with ads to an excessive degree or that make it hard to find the actual original content on the page."*

Sneaky links in footers, headers or elsewhere

Does your site have links in the footer?

Links *per se* are not a problem, but if they are links with keyword rich anchor text, they could be. If the links in your footer are there simply to make another webpage rank better for a keyword term, then there is a problem.

Look at your footer links. Do they use keyword rich anchor text that the linked to page wants to rank for? If so, remove them.

If you have other footer links to things like Twitter, Facebook, Contact, Privacy etc, then these are fine.

Web page real estate checklist

• Resize your browser to 1024x768 and see what loads above the fold. Is there useful content? Are there too many adverts? If there are too many adverts, especially above the fold, consider removing (or moving) them.

• If you removed all of the adverts from the pages on your site, would those pages still offer the visitor what they are looking for? If not, then the content is not good enough.

• Does your site have sneaky links in the footer, especially keyword rich anchor text links to your own site or an external site? If so, get rid of them.

Checklist Point #3 – Site structure

Is your site navigation helping your visitors find what they want quickly?

If you think in terms of needing every page on your site to be just 1 and a maximum of 2 clicks away from the homepage, then you're on the right track.

Good website navigation should be intuitive to the visitor. They should immediately be able to see where they need to go for the information they require.

A good test here is to ask a friend who has never been to your website to find a particular piece of information. How long does it take them?

Include a search box

I'd highly recommend you have a search box on your website to help people find information. If you are using WordPress, the default search box really is very poor. People won't be able to find what they want on a large site because WordPress doesn't rank its results by any kind of relevance (at least not any that I can detect).

An example

On one of my websites, I had written an article on "vitamin A". I had also referenced vitamin A in 120+ other articles on the site. The WordPress search box placed my main "vitamin A" article around position 125. That's not very good!

WordPress or not, check out the search script your site is using. Do some searches. Does it return the most relevant pages in the results for search queries? If the results are not very good, then you need to look for a new search box script. There is one I can recommend.

What if you could use Google's search engine to power the search box on your site?

Google are kings of search and relevance, so using a search box powered by Google would ensure people find the most relevant pages on your site, quickly and easily. The good news is you can. After installing it on the site I mentioned above, and searching for "vitamin A", my main article came up #1, just as it should do.

You can find out more about Google Custom Search here:

http://www.google.com/cse/

If you have an AdSense account, you can create the search box within that account to use on your site. It will have AdSense ads in the search results, but you do make money when the adverts are clicked. If you want to opt-out of the adverts in your custom search engine, visit the link above because Google do have a paid option for this.

Site-wide links

Site-wide links are links that appear on all pages of your site. You do actually have to be careful and not overdo them. If you do have site-wide links, they should not use keyword phrases you are trying to rank for.

NOTE: Site-wide links can be to pages on your own website or a different website.

In the past, swapping site-wide links with webmasters of other sites has been a common SEO practice, but I am saying don't do it. Google's quality guidelines clearly state that IF these are an attempt to manipulate search rankings, then they should be avoided.

If you are a WordPress site owner, typical site-wide links that comes pre-installed with WordPress include the blogroll. I recommend you remove this from your site, even if you have edited it with more relevant websites.

Site-wide links are typically found in the header, footer or sidebar of the site. One of the most common forms of site-wide links is the main menu of the site. This menu links to the main areas of the website and serves a useful purpose. I would recommend that your main navigation menu is not keyword-focused, and instead, is written with the visitor in mind to help them find what they are looking for.

On smaller sites (10 or so pages), the main navigation menu usually links to all of the pages on the site. Again, avoid keyword-rich anchor text in these menus and always think what is most helpful to the visitor.

As your site grows, it becomes unnatural to link to all pages on your site from the main menu found on every page. A far better strategy is to create individual menus for each section of your site, and put these menus on the pages in those sections. Let's consider "context-sensitive navigation".

Context-sensitive navigation

The navigation system on your site can include menus in:

• The header

• The footer

• The sidebar

• Within the content area, usually at the end of a particular piece of content.

On larger websites, the navigation system you use should not be the same on every page of the site. The navigation should change depending on the page being visited. I'm not suggesting every page on your site has a different navigation menu, but certainly sections of your site could use their own custom menu.

The easiest way to think about this is with an example. If you had a health site, and the visitor is on a page about osteoporosis, a menu that could help the visitor would contain links to other articles about osteoporosis. You could still include a navigation "block" linking to the main areas within the site, but you'd also include more specific options for your visitor, related to the current article they are reading.

Let's consider another example. If you had a travel site and a visitor was on a page talking about restaurants in Bali, it would make sense to have navigation options that show other articles on Bali, maybe hotels, attractions, surfing, etc.

What if you have an ecommerce site selling baby products? You might have a main site-wide menu that includes links to all of the main sections on your site – strollers, cots, car seats, etc, but when your visitor is browsing the section on strollers, a menu with links to 2-seat strollers, jogging strollers, etc would be very helpful. Always think in terms of how your navigation can best serve your visitors.

This type of dynamic navigation is clearly easier and more practical to implement on larger sites. However, if you have a small site with a site-wide menu, do look at your navigation and make sure your links are not keyword-focused and that the navigation HELPS the visitor.

A tip for WordPress users

Two plugins I recommend for helping you create a dynamic navigation system are:

• **Dynamic widgets**. (http://bit.ly/7472kF). This allows you to setup different sidebar menus (created as widgets) in different areas of your site.

• **Yet Another Related Posts Plugin (YARPP).** (http://bit.ly/uN6WD). This allows you to setup a related posts section after each piece of content. When a visitor gets to the end of an article, they'll see a list of related articles and be tempted to click through to one. This type of internal linking is also beneficial from a search engine perspective as it links related content together.

Content organization on your server (non-WordPress sites)

Organization of your content on the server and your site's navigation system go hand-in-hand. One mirrors the other. Well organized content is stored in a logical, intuitive manner, which is reflected in the navigation system.

The physical organization on your server is only important if you are building your website using something like HTML, which stores as webpage as a discrete file. It therefore doesn't apply to WordPress (WordPress does not save content as individual files).

Let's use a theoretical example of a pet website. It might have content written about:

- Fish
- Birds
- Dogs
- Reptiles
- Amphibians
- Cats

There should be a folder/directory on your server for each of these content areas, and all content should be saved into the corresponding folder. Can you see how this physical organization would mirror the navigation system of the site?

The first thing for you to check is whether or not your content is properly organized into folders on your server. Are all dog related articles physically located within a dog folder (aka a directory) on your server?

As the dog section on the site grows, we'll need to add to the structure of the folders/directories on our server to re-organize our content, in the exact same way that we did with the navigation system earlier.

For example, if your site was an informational site, you could add the following sub-folders under your "dog" folder on the server:

- Training
- Toys
- Beds
- Food & treats

Each of these would then store the content related to those folders. So for example, all articles on dog training would be located in the "/dogs/training/" folder on your server.

If your site sold pets, perhaps a more logical way to organize the content would be to have sub-folders like:

- Alsatians
- Terriers
- Dalmatians

- Huskies

.. And so on.

By organizing your content into logical folders on your server, the URLs of these pages would be like this:

mypetsite.com/**dogs/training/**clickers.html

mypetsite.com/**dogs/training/**choke-chain.html

mypetsite.com/**dogs/training/**walking-to-heel.html

mypetsite.com/**dogs/food/**mixers.html

mypetsite.com/**dogs/food/**tinned-dog-food.html

mypetsite.com/**dogs/food/**snacks.html

These URLs give the search engines big clues about the content. For example, the search engines would know that all 6 of those web pages were about dogs. It would also know that three were related to training dogs, while three were related to dog food.

This type of physical organization helps the search engines categorize and rank your content because your pages end up in "silos" of related content (with links between related content).

This folder organization on your server should match the menu navigation on your site.

NOTE: If you are using WordPress, you can get the same types of URLs by using categories. While categories are not physical locations like directories/folders on the server, the do serve the same purpose in categorizing your content into logical groups.

WordPress actually takes things a stage further and includes a feature called tags. You can think of tags as an additional way to classify your content, the main way being with categories. I won't go into how to use WordPress categories and tags in this book, other than to give you two quick tips:

1. Never use a word or phrase as both a category and a tag. If it's a really important part of your site structure it's a category. If it's less important, use a tag.
2. Never use a tag if it will only ever be used on one post. If a tag is important, it will be used on several posts on your site. If it's not, it's not important, therefore delete it.

Internal linking of content

When one of your pieces of content references information that is found somewhere else on your site, it makes sense to link to that other page within the body of your content. If we look at this Wikipedia page you can see a lot of links:

Although oxidation reactions are crucial for life, they can also be damaging; plants and animals maintain complex systems of multiple types of antioxidants, such as glutathione, vitamin C, vitamin A, and vitamin E as well as enzymes such as catalase, superoxide dismutase and various peroxidases. Insufficient levels of antioxidants, or inhibition of the antioxidant enzymes, cause oxidative stress and may damage or kill cells.

Substituted phenols and derivatives of phenylenediamine are common antioxidants used to inhibit gum formation in gasoline (petrol).

Each of these links goes to another web page on the Wikipedia website. I've circled one hyperlink where the anchor text is "glutathione". This link jumps to the page on Wikipedia all about "glutathione". Not only does this help the search engine spider to index the pages on your site, it also helps the visitor to navigate more easily. Anyone reading this article that doesn't know what glutathione is could click the link and read about it before returning to the original page to continue reading.

Internal linking helps visitors, and it also help the search engines. Links with anchor text tell the search engine what the page is about. The only recommendation I'd make with internal linking is that you vary the anchor text in those links, much like you do with external links pointing into your website.

I did an experiment on internal linking and published my results here on my site:

http://bit.ly/SttMWD

The article gives you tips on using internal linking, plus results of an experiment I ran.

Essentially I took one of my websites that ranked at #190 for a particular phrase I was targeting. Using nothing but internal links, I managed to move that page up to #14 in Google. That to me indicates that Google like internal linking when it's done to help the visitor (and it clearly helps your pages rank better).

The things I'd recommend you look at on your own site are:

1. Do you make use of internal linking in the body of the content like Wikipedia?
2. Do you vary internal link anchor texts to a specific page?
3. For any particular anchor text, make sure you only ever link to one URL using it. Using the same anchor text to point to two or more different URLs is confusing, especially for the search engines.

Site structure checklist

• Is your navigation intuitive?

• Are all of the pages on your site just one or two clicks away from the homepage?

• Do you have site-wide links in the sidebar?

• Do you have site-wide links in the header?

• Do you have site-wide links in the footer?

NOTE: Site-wide links with keyword-rich anchor text are the most potentially damaging.

• If you have a large site, do you use dynamic menus, which change depending on the section of the site the visitor is viewing?

• Do you have a search box? If it is a WordPress default search box, I highly recommend you switch to a more efficient script, e.g. Google's custom search.

• Do you internally link the pages of your website from within the body of your content, not just via the navigation menus or a related posts menu?

• Is your content organized logically into "silos" where all related content is in the same category or folder? If necessary (e.g. on a large site), do you use sub-folders to help make the navigation even more intuitive?

• If you are using WordPress, do you have tags that are only used once or twice? If so, remove them.

• If you are using WordPress, do you have tags that are identical to some of your categories? Never use a phrase for a tag if it is being used (or will be used) as a category.

Checklist Point #4 – Comments

Visitor contact

A visitor-friendly site is one that offers your visitors the chance to interact with you.

Something ALL websites should have is a contact form.

Something else that I highly recommend you include is a comment form where visitors can comment on your content. Obviously, this may not be applicable in all cases, but visitors do like to know there is a real person behind a site and often like to give their opinions as well. Not only does a comment form build trust, it also builds social proof as new visitors can see that other people have left comments on your site.

There are contact form scripts and comment form scripts available for HTML websites. Content management systems like WordPress have the comments built in, and contact forms are readily available as plugins.

I recommend you implement both on your site if it makes sense to do so.

If you already have a comment form on your site, check the comment settings. If you have your comments set to auto-approve, then set it to "administrator approval" so that ALL comments need to go by you first. If you set up comments for auto-approval, you'll get a lot of spam comments that bring the quality of your site down, and could themselves cause a penalty if these comments link to "bad neighborhoods".

Bad neighborhoods?

Let me explain.

Most spammers leave comments with the sole intention of getting a backlink to their own web site. Many of these will be low quality sites, porn sites, or other types of sites that you would not want to associate with your own. These types of sites are referred to as "bad neighborhoods" by Google. In addition, there is nothing to stop someone who has left a comment on your site (and had it approved some time ago), from redirecting their link to a bad neighborhood at a later date. To be safe, make comments on your site **nofollow**.

Once everything is set up properly, go through **every single comment** on your site and delete any that are either fake or spam.

Fake comments

Fake comments are those that you or someone you asked (or hired) wrote. A lot of webmasters add fake comments to their own site to make the site look a little more active.

Don't do it. Fake comments are often easily spotted and don't instill trust once you've been rumbled.

Typical ways that fake comments stand out are:

1. Several comments posted within a very short time of one another and then nothing, at least for a while.
2. Groups of fake comments rarely have author images associated with the comment (Gravatars) which makes them stand out even more.
3. Comments are "bland" and don't really add anything to the content.
4. Comments are copied from another website, e.g. Amazon.

Spam comments

Spam comments are not always easy to spot. They are left with the sole intention of getting a valuable backlink, so spammers have become creative in the way they do their spamming. There are even software tools to help them carry out mass-scale spamming of comment-enabled websites.

As a general rule, don't approve any comment that is "stroking your ego", or "patting you on the back for a job well done".

One way spammers try to get their comments approved is to say things like "Great article" or "This is amazing, I've told my friends about this". Here is one I got the other day:

> Submitted on 2013/03/05 at 08:42
>
> You blog post is just completely quality and informative. Many new facts and information which I have not heard about before. Keep sharing more blog posts.

While I have no doubt that this comment is true ;) sadly it is spam.

This flattery is supposed to stroke the ego of the webmaster so it gets through the approval process. Don't approve it, UNLESS you know the comment is legitimate i.e. you recognize the commenter.

Comment spam can also be cleverly disguised.

For example, a spammer might find a page they want a backlink from on the "health benefits of zinc". They'll then go and find an article on the web about this topic and grab a quote from that article to use as a comment. The quote will look like a real comment about your article, but will in fact be content copied from another website. This type is often difficult to catch, except to say that most cases don't quite look right in the context of your article. If in doubt, grab the content of the comments, put it in quotes, and search Google for it.

Another type of comment spam is where the commenter is just trying to get traffic to their own website. Here is an example of that:

> Submitted on 2013/03/08 at 13:34
>
> I would certainly not recommend 1&1. My recent experiences are detailed on my blog, here;
>
> I have always found Bluehost easy to use, Hostgator I find a little "clunky" but my favourite has to be Dreamhost. They had a few issues in the past but everything works like a dream for me and I find their unique control panel interface so easy to use.

You can see I've blurred out the URL linking to his web page.

His page is basically a review of his favorite web hosting company (which does include his experiences with 1&1), and an affiliate link to that host. He left a comment that I would have otherwise approved, but not with that link to his web page. He is probably targeting any "high traffic" website that has reviewed the 1&1 web host, or even Hostgator, and leaving similar reviews in the hope he can piggy-back their traffic as well as benefit from the relevant backlink.

General rule for approving comments

Only approve comments if:

1. It is clear from the comment that the person has read the article.
2. The comment adds something to the article, like another point of view.
3. If you know that the person is real because you recognize their name (but only if the comment is also not spammy).

Obviously these are just guidelines. In the field of battle, you'll have to make some tough decisions, but I recommend only keeping the best comments that you're sure are genuine. Delete EVERYTHING else.

Comments checklist

• Does your website have a comments section where visitors can leave comments, thoughts and questions?

• Does your website have a contact us form?

• If you have comments enabled, are you manually approving all comments? You should be.

• Check through all of the comments on your site and remove any fake or spam comments. In fact, remove any comment whose sole purpose is to get a backlink to a website.

• Make comment links nofollow.

• Going forward, only approve legitimate comments where it is clear the visitor has read your content and added to the conversation with their insight.

Checklist Point #5 – Social presence

Under the umbrella of social presence, I include two things:

• The website/website author has a social presence on social media sites.

• The website has social sharing "buttons" on the site to allow visitors to share the content to their social media followers.

Check your website. Do you have both of these?

Let's look to see exactly what I mean, as well as give you some ideas for a "bare minimum" social approach.

The website/website author has a social presence

The three main social channels I'd recommend you look at are:

1. Facebook
2. Twitter
3. Google Plus

I would probably recommend you consider these in that order as well. If you have a Facebook account you can easily setup a Facebook Page for your website. You can then link to the Facebook page from your site.

You can see how I have this setup on one of my sites. Visitors can follow me on Twitter, Facebook or add me to a circle on Google plus.

Your Facebook page offers your visitors an additional channel for starting a "conversation" with you. From your point of view, you can post updates to that page which include things like:

• Tips and tricks for your industry/niche.

• Current news in your niche.

• Interesting articles you find around the web.

• New posts on your site (this can be automated).

• Videos, images etc.

• Current special offers from your website.

• Anything else that is relevant to your site and niche.

Think of your Facebook page as an extension of your website. A Facebook page that has a thriving community can rank well in Google, plus give your "brand" a huge amount of social proof. It's so easy to setup, I recommend all websites have a Facebook page.

As far as Twitter is concerned, it's also very easy to setup an account for your website. You can even setup your website to automatically send a tweet to your Twitter account, every time new content is published on your site. You can of course also send tweets with information related to your niche (the same kind of stuff that you can post on Facebook). Services like Hootsuite (http://hootsuite.com) allow you to schedule tweets (as well as Facebook and Google Plus posts) in advance.

As your Twitter following increases, you'll automatically be increasing your "authority" in the eyes of your visitors. Let's face it, if you have a Twitter account with 10,000+ followers, a lot of people will think "Wow, this site must be good".

Now, before you tell me that you've tried Twitter and only ever managed to get a handful of followers, there are ways to increase the number of followers. I wrote an article called "How to get more Twitter Followers" (http://bit.ly/QC0PaT) and I have used the methods described there to consistently build Twitter lists into the thousands. While it's true that your Twitter list may not be too responsive when built that way, that's not really the point. The main point of this to begin with is social proof on your site. As your site grows in authority, your Twitter following will increase naturally with more targeted individuals. It then becomes more than just a social proof thing. It becomes a useful tool for business.

When you have a Twitter account, make sure you link to it from your website so that people can follow you on Twitter (as I did in the previous screenshot). Once your Twitter following has grown to the point where you are proud of it, you may want to head on over to http://twittercounter.com and get a "badge" for your site. The badge displays how many Twitter followers you've got. This all helps add authority to your site, and the more authority your site is given by visitors, the more authority it is given by the search engines which monitor visitor behavior.

The final social media platform that I recommend getting involved with is Google Plus. You can setup a Google Plus "Page" for your website and post to it, in much the same way you do to

Facebook. Google plus works in a very different way though, and it's beyond the scope of this book to teach you Google Plus.

As a bare minimum, I'd recommend you setup Google Authorship for your website, and for this, you need a Google plus account. Essentially the way this works is that you tell Google which web content you own, and they credit you as the author. Obviously they need to verify this, but that is all part of the setup procedure.

Setting up Google Authorship can help in two main ways:

1. When you publish content on your site, you are tagged as the original owner. If anyone else steals your content, Google knows that YOU are the original owner; therefore you aren't likely to be outranked by a thief.
2. Your Avatar can show up in the search results next to your entry, which can increase your click through rate and increases your authority in the eyes of the searchers. Here is an example of how this looks in Google:

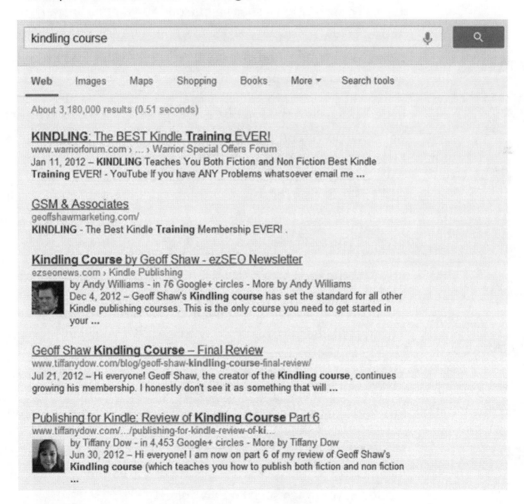

Do you see how both my entry and that of Tiffany Dow stick out from the others? Our rankings encourage the click and add authority to our listing. It's like Google are saying, "Hey, look! These people (that we know), have an article on this".

Setting up Google Authorship is beyond the scope of this book, but Google have help pages that can guide you through the setup procedure:

https://plus.google.com/authorship

OK, those are the social media channels that I suggest you get involved in.

Let's see how you can give your visitors the opportunity to share your content with their followers – using social sharing buttons.

The website has social sharing "buttons"

If I show you an example, I am sure you'll recognize what I am talking about.

Typically, social media sharing buttons appear in a "panel", either above, below (or above AND below) the content on the page. This panel can be horizontal or even floating vertically (as in the screenshot above), over the webpage on the right or left, or in a sidebar.

In my screenshot, the top one is Facebook, the second Twitter and the third Google Plus. Again, I'd recommend concentrating on these three.

NOTE: The bottom one in the screenshot is another service called Buffer, which isn't currently on my essential list. It could be in the future though, so you may want to read up on that service here:

http://bufferapp.com/

Other social media sites you might like to have buttons for include Pinterest (if your site has a lot of images that you want shared) and StumbleUpon.

For WordPress users, there are a stack of plugins to add this functionality to a site.

For HTML sites, you'll need to find a script that has these features, or manually go to each social media site and grab the button code to include in your own social media "panel".

What do these buttons do exactly?

These buttons give visitors to your site the opportunity to share your webpage with their social media followers.

For example, if I clicked on the Tweet button in the panel above, a Tweet would be constructed automatically with the URL and title of that page.

You'll see at the end of the Tweet that Twitter has added "via @KISSmetrics". This sends "KISSmetrics" (the author of the content) a notification that I have tweeted their content. This is one way you can connect with the leaders in your niche.

When you have these social share buttons on your site, your visitors become your army of promoters, as long as your content is good.

So, check your site. Do you have social sharing buttons? If not, I highly recommend you add them (at least for the main three).

NOTE: Google do index tweets and probably use them as a social signal in ranking (although probably only for a limited time). Google also knows how many Facebook likes your content gets and may use that as a social signal. And of course, Google obviously monitor Google pluses.

Social presence checklist

• Does the website have a presence on Facebook?

• Does the website have a presence on Twitter?

• Does the website have a presence on Google plus?

105

• Does your website have social sharing buttons that allow your visitors to share your content with their social media followers? You should include Twitter, Facebook and Google plus as a bare minimum.

• Setup Google Authorship for your site, connecting your content to your Google plus profile.

Checklist Point #6 – Would you trust the site?

This section looks at the trust levels for your site. We've already discussed some of the things that can help people trust your site, but let's look at a more comprehensive list.

People like to deal with real people. So when they arrive at your site, do they know who they are dealing with?

A photo

A lot of split testing has shown that a photo of a real person increases conversions. From my own experience, the photos that work the best are NOT the ones that look like "stock photos", but those that look like a real person, the person next door. There's a reason for that. Websites that show real people help to build trust. When someone trusts your site, they are more likely to follow through with your call to action.

So where are the best places to put a photo on your site? Well it really depends on the type of site you have, but a photo in the header or the sidebar can work. Here is one found in a sidebar:

Do you see how Shane looks like a real person in that photo?

Incidentally, Shane is a friend of mine who created a social media plugin for WordPress sites called **Social Essentials** (http://bit.ly/GTCfPJ). You might like to check it out to help you with that last section on social media presence.

The style of Shane's photo is very different from many of the photo's you'd get from a stock photo site:

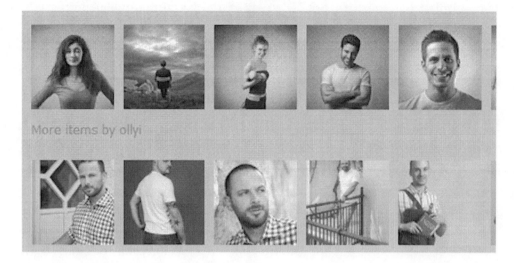

Whichever photo you use, make sure you look like a real person and not a photographic model. People want to trust the photo and anything that looks too glitzy could be seen as fake.

My favorite place to include a photo is in an author's resource box at the end of each piece of content. Here is an example:

There's a separate case in progress that may lead to the Microsoft patent being ruled invalid, but that doesn't appear to have any bearing on this case at the moment.

A final decision is expected in May.

Related Entries
- Google In Privacy Flap With Germans Over New iOS Maps
- Google, Microsoft Cooperate To Invalidate Broad Online Mapping Patent

Related Topics: Google: Legal | Google: Maps & Local | Google: Outside US | Legal: Patents | Top News

 About The Author: Matt McGee is Editor-In-Chief of Search Engine Land. His news career includes time spent in TV, radio, and print journalism. His web career continues to include a small number of SEO and social media consulting clients, as well as regular speaking engagements at marketing events around the U.S. He blogs at Small Business Search Marketing and can be found on Twitter at @MattMcGee and/or on Google Plus. You can read Matt's disclosures on his personal blog. See more articles by Matt McGee

Connect with the author via: Email | Twitter | Google+ | LinkedIn

This author box is at the end of the article. Notice also how there are links to his social channels underneath.

If you don't have a photograph of the author or owner on your site, I'd recommend you add one ASAP.

About Us page

Every website should have an About Us page and those that do, often find it's one of the most visited pages on the site. The About Us page is something that many of us skip over and ignore, but it really does help to build trust when people can find out more about you and your site. It also gives you an opportunity to let your visitors understand you on a more human level. What drives you and the site? That can be very important on dry, technical types of sites. If you want more advice on how to create an "About Us" page, I recommend you read this article:

http://bit.ly/UNPgVb

Bryan Eisenberg offers some great advice and even gets you started by answering some simple questions.

Comments enabled

We've already talked about comments earlier in this book. Make sure you have a comment system installed on your site so that visitors can leave feedback. Good feedback can only help build trust and social proof for you and your brand.

Does the site pretend to be a merchant?

This specifically refers to affiliate sites who send traffic to a merchant site in return for making commissions on any sale.

Some affiliate marketers don't make it clear that they are an intermediary in the sales process, rather than the actual merchant.

E.g. the marketers may use links that say "Buy here" or "Buy now" without letting customers know they'll be visiting a different site to complete the transaction. Look at it from a visitor point of view. Don't you think it's a bit of a shock to be on one site, click the "buy" button, and then end up on say Amazon, for example? Sure it is.

Is the site/webmaster a recognized authority?

Being an authority basically means you are recognized as someone to trust in your niche. It's something you can achieve relatively easily if you do one thing:

BE EVERYWHERE!

Part of the reason I look for a social presence from the websites I critique is because these help to build your authority. If someone finds your Facebook page (where they see your photo) in Google, and likes it, then when they go to your website (and see your photo) they think, "hmmm, I've seen this person before and they know what they're talking about." The same goes for any social media channel (as long as you only share quality information to those channels).

One method I use to extend my reach into a niche is to use the same photograph (either me, or the persona for that site), on my site, my Facebook, Twitter & Google+ pages, PLUS, and this is a big one, as a **Gravatar** (http://en.gravatar.com/), which is set up on the main email address for the site. A Gravatar is just an image associated with an email address. Whenever you post on forums, or comment on Gravatar-enabled blogs, your photo is shown next to your post. People will start to recognize you everywhere they go within that niche, because you are "Everywhere". If the information your share through these channels is good, you can quickly build a reputation as someone to trust, an authority figure in your niche.

NOTE: Being a recognized authority is particularly important on medical sites. You need to know what you are talking about first and foremost, but secondly, people need to trust you. If you are a doctor, or have specific training related to your site, let your visitors know.

If your site is related to health or medicine, are you a recognized authority? If not, then that is something you might like to work on.

Other reasons people don't trust your website?
There are a few other reasons why people won't trust a website. I won't go into details on each of these reasons, I'll just list them. If they are missing from your own website, then maybe you'll consider adding them.

• No Contact page.

• No privacy page.

• No business address or phone number clearly displayed.

• Doesn't seem to have been updated in years.

• No testimonials.

• Copyright notice on the website is out of date.

• Lack of "trust symbols", e.g. Better Business Bureau, VeriSign, McAfee, etc.

• Web pages with typos, spelling mistakes or grammatical errors.

• Lack of response from YOU where comments/questions have been posted.

• Bad reviews.

• Poorly targeted emails, and difficulty unsubscribing from your newsletter.

Trust checklist

• Does the site have a photo of the webmaster/author of the content?

• Does your site have an About Us page?

• Are Comments enabled?

• Does your site pretend to be a merchant?

• Is the author of your site a recognized authority in the niche/industry?

• Are you using a Gravatar setup on the email address you use for your site?

• Is your business address displayed on the site, preferably with a phone number?

• When was the last time your site was updated?

• If appropriate, are there testimonials and are they up to date?

• Does the copyright notice on your website display the correct year?

• Do you display any trust symbols (if appropriate)

• Check all content for spellings and grammatical errors. Check your navigation systems for these errors as well.

• Are there unanswered comments on your site?

Checklist Point #7 – Bounce rates & time on site

There are two metrics that Google most certainly monitor as a way of determining visitor satisfaction levels. The first is the bounce rate and the second is the time they spend on your site.

According to Google:

> *"Bounce rate is the percentage of visits that go only one page before exiting a site."*

In other words, someone only views one page on your site before exiting. Typically, high bounce rates are seen as bad. It may mean that people are not finding what they want on your site.

Time on site is the length of time a visitor stays on your site. A low time on site may indicate a problem with your content, since people aren't sticking around to read it.

The problem is, Google Analytics does not accurately report bounce rates or time on site. Rather than explain, you can read this article on the topic which also contains a fix:

http://bit.ly/KbUvs9

I recommend you implement the change suggested in that article. You'll then have a better idea of your true bounce rates and visitor time on site.

Once the change is set up, leave your site to collect new data for a month or so before trying to analyze these metrics. Then, go through your analytics to find pages that have high bounce rates AND low time spent on the page(s).

A page with a high bounce rate but high time on the page is not a problem. Look at these examples:

Avg. Time on Page	Entrances	Bounce Rate ↓
00:52:18	3	66.67%
00:00:00	2	50.00%
00:17:41	2	50.00%
00:00:00	4	50.00%

The top page in the list has a bounce rate of 66.67% (the site average is around 10% so 66.67% is high). Despite the high bounce rate, I am happy with this page because there were three visitors, with an average time on that page of 52 minutes 18 seconds. This tells me that the visitor must have found the information useful and engaging.

Similarly, the second page I highlighted above has a bounce rate of 50% with two visits. However, the average time on that page was 17 minutes 41 seconds, so again, those two visitors must have found what they wanted (or at least found it interesting) before they hit their back button to go back to Google.

The two pages that would worry me are the examples that I haven't circled. Both pages had an average time on site of 0 minutes. I would go and look at these pages in more depth, and over a longer period of time, to see whether there may have been a glitch in the reporting during the above screenshot, or whether these pages historically have high bounce rates and a low time on the page.

What you need to so is identify pages with high bounce rate AND low time on the page and see if you can work out why visitors are not satisfied with what they see. If the content is good, maybe it's just not a good match for the search phrase they used to find you in Google. Maybe something else is pushing them away from your site? You need to look for ways to increase the visitor time on these pages (and hopefully decrease bounce rate).

Bounce rate & time on site checklist

I recommend you install the updated code here (which will give you a more accurate measurement of these parameters):

http://bit.ly/KbUvs9

Once installed and allowed to run for a few weeks, check your bounce rate and time on site at Google Analytics.

• Are your average bounce rates high?

• Are visitors spending a long or short time on your site?

• Look for specific pages where bounce rate is high AND time on site is low. Try to work out why these pages are suffering and fix them accordingly.

Checklist Point #8 – Legal pages

There are certain pages on a website that I call "legal" pages. These are things like:

• Privacy

• Disclaimers (including any medical or earnings disclaimers).

• Contact Us

• Terms

• About Us (we talked about this earlier in terms of visitor trust).

• Any other documents that should be displayed on your site. These might include things like cookie policy, anti-spam policy, outbound link disclaimer and so on.

Does your website include all of the necessary documents?

This article will help you decide which legal documents you need:

http://bit.ly/10gf6y5

They also offer webmasters free "legal" documents here:

http://bit.ly/MDyCmd

There are "credits" written into these documents that need to be left in place, but for a small fee (currently £3.50), you can get that credit removed.

Legal pages checklist

Not all of these pages are necessary for all types of website, so check which pages your site needs and add them if they are missing.

• Do you have a privacy page?

• Do you have a disclaimer page?

• Do you have a terms of use and conditions page (TOS)?

• Do you have a contact page?

• Do you have an about us page?

• Do you have a medical disclaimer page?

• Do you have an email policy page?

• Do you have an outbound link policy page?

Checklist Point #9 – Content quality

This is a huge component of modern SEO.

If your content is bad, then getting everything else right won't fix the site.

You need to have a website that you are proud of. More than that, you need to have a website that you would be proud to show anyone at Google. Content is what separates an average site from a great site and the best way to understand what Google is looking for is to ask yourself:

"Could the content appear in a magazine?"

This question was actually taken from the Google blog when discussing quality content, so it's what you should be aiming for.

Obviously ecommerce sites have a lot of pages that wouldn't satisfy this question, but it's a great question to ask on any article-based content.

Here is another question that can apply to most types of content:

"Is your content the type of content that people will want to bookmark, or share socially?"

NOTE: Google can certainly detect bookmarks and social shares, so they are able to use them as indicators if they choose to.

The biggest problem I have found concerning content quality is that webmasters are not very impartial when judging their own. If you can, it's always better to get someone else to evaluate your content.

Besides the quality of your content, there are a number of things to look out for as you assess the content on your website. Here is a checklist (in no particular order):

• Has the content been copied and published by other websites?

This is a common problem, though setting up Google Authorship for your site should keep your content safer moving forward. To check whether your content has been stolen, you could use a site like **Copyscape** (http://www.copyscape.com). Alternatively, grab a sentence or two from your web page and search for it on Google between quotes. Google will then tell you whether that text is found on any other website(s).

Here is an example of what it looks like when you do this type of search and other sites have copied your content:

See how there are 9 results in Google, each with the identical text.

If other sites have stolen your content and used it on their own sites, I'd recommend setting up Google authorship immediately, if you haven't already. Next, contact those other sites and ask them to take the content down as it's breaching your copyright. Usually the threat of getting their hosting company involved is enough for most people to remove your stuff. Here is an article written by Jim Edwards that addresses the problem of copyright infringement:

http://bit.ly/13sbuNV

The article is a little old, but it still has great advice.

If you prefer, you can hire services to deal with content thieves. http://www.dmca.com is one; although I've never used them, so cannot personally vouch for their service.

• Product reviews unbiased?

If you have product reviews on your site, are they unbiased, or positive, positive and more hyped up positives? You need to share both sides of the story and ALL products have some things that are not perfect.

• More than just a rehash of the merchant site content?

On the topic of reviews, is the content just a rehash of what you can find on the merchant site or perhaps Amazon? Your reviews need to be PERSONAL.   Readers must know that you have personally tried the product and therefore your review must contain insights not seen on ANY other website. Write your review from personal experience.

• Affiliate link disclaimer?

If your site is an affiliate site, do you have an affiliate link disclaimer? Do people on your site know you are not the merchant?

This all comes back to the issue of trust. I realize that an affiliate link disclaimer can hurt conversion rates, so try to find a way to tell your visitors in such a way that they don't mind you being an affiliate. After all, you are helping them with their buying decision, aren't you?

In my experience, if someone reads an impartial review that was obviously written by someone that had used the product, they don't mind clicking a link knowing it's an affiliate link. If they read a hyped up sales pitch and then find out your link is an affiliate link, then good luck with that.

• Keyword stuffing

Keyword stuffing is a really bad SEO crime. In the past, webmaster knew that adding keywords to their content would make it rank better for those keywords, and articles often became stuffed with keyword phrases. Today, that kind of thing will get your site penalized or even booted out of Google altogether.

As you read your content, ask yourself if it was written for a human or a search engine. If the latter, then re-write it or scrap it altogether.

A quick test for stuffing is to read your content carefully (or get a friend to read it). Can you pick out phrases you think the article was designed to rank for because of the way it repeats a phrase, or slight grammatical errors that were left in just so a particular phrase could be inserted?

All keyword stuffed content MUST be removed. Whether that means re-writing it or deleting it, that's your choice.

My advice when you are writing content is WRITE NATURALLY!

If you hear anyone talking about keyword densities, ignore them. The correct density for any word or phrase on a page is the density that it ends up as when written naturally. It might be 2%, it might be 1%, and it might even be 0.1% or 0%. Bear that in mind. As you read your content, try to see if any word or phrase seems to be used more than is natural.

• **Fluff rating**

Fluff rating is a term I use with my students.

Looking at the http://www.thefreedictionary.com/fluff, fluff is defined as:

> ***Something of little substance or consequence***, *especially:*
>
> *a. Light or superficial entertainment: The movie was just another bit of fluff from Hollywood.*
>
> *b. **Inflated or padded material: The report was mostly fluff, with little new information.***

Part (b) is exactly what I am referring to - an article that goes on and on but doesn't really say anything.

Webmasters have typically tried to increase the length of their content because they think that longer content ranks better. This means that an article that could be covered in just 400 words in a quality piece is stretched out to 600 words - 200 of which are fluff, and only there to raise the word count.

Fluffy content is often found on websites that outsource their content creation. The webmaster asks the writer for a certain word count (since articles are bought on a per word basis), so may request a 600 word article, irrespective of whether the topic NEEDS 600 words or not. The writer then struggles to find 600 words worth of content, so pads it out with fluff.

An article that says very little despite the word count, has a high fluff rating and should be deleted or re-written to provide quality information on a given topic.

• Information duplicated on multiple articles

Does information on one page of your site appear on other pages as well? In other words, is there overlap between the content on the various pages of your site? If so, you need to remove it. If two or more articles are closely related enough to share the same information, consider merging those pieces into one big article.

The pages on a website should all contain different information and there should be a bare minimum of content overlap.

• Check the sitemap

A sitemap is a great way to check your content. As you look through the sitemap, are there instances where two pages have very similar filenames, or titles? If so, are those two pages covering the same information? If yes, consider combining them into a single quality article?

A common strategy for building a website is to carry out keyword research and then write content around the keywords that have high demand and low competition. One problem with this approach is that two or more phrases - that basically mean the same thing - often become the basis for separate articles.

A site might have separate articles based on each of these phrases:

• Best vacuum

• Best vacuum cleaner

• Which is the best vacuum?

Can you see how those three phrases are saying the same thing? So how can there be three separate articles for these phrases?

Here is an example I found on one website:

This website has an article on "room addition" and another on "room additions". Really?

Here is another example:

> The mood of the party is set right at the beginning.
>
> ### Baby Shower Invitation Idea
> Here is a fun baby shower invitation idea to help cr
> occasion.
>
> ### Baby Shower Invitation
> A great baby shower invitation for the internet age.
>
> ### Baby Shower Invite
> Since the baby shower invite is the grand introduci
> with it.

Do those three articles on baby shower invitations really have useful, unique content without fluff? If I was critiquing this site, this would be the kind of thing I would be looking for on the sitemap as clues of content problems.

What about these two pages found on the same site:

> Many companies now offer beautiful satin baby shower invitations.
>
> #### Baby Shower Invitations For Twins
> Double the blessing and a baby shower invitations for twins should convey the excitement.
>
> #### Twin Baby Shower Invitation
> A twin baby shower invitation has the added feat of acknowledging more than one gender.

The reason webmasters do this is not for the benefit of the visitor. It's for the benefit of the search engine. They hope that each page will rank well for its variation of the phrase, and therefore bring a lot more traffic to the site than just one article optimized for one of the phrases.

Today, this type of keyword focused content will get your site into trouble, so check through your sitemap to identify possible problems. You can combine similar articles into one, but make sure you cut the fluff and make these articles the best they can be.

• Titles & headlines

The <title> tag is an important part of a webpage as it tells the visitor what the page is about (the title is often used in Google as the anchor text to the page). The headline on the page is also important for similar reasons. Google has traditionally used keywords in the title and headlines to help rank a page, so yes, you guessed it, webmasters have abused these areas.

1. Your titles should be written for HUMANS, not search engines.
2. Your headlines should be written for HUMANS, not search engines (are you seeing a pattern here?).
3. Your title and headline should not be the same on any particular page.
4. No two pages should share the same title.

In the past, one of the best ways to rank a page for a particular phrase was to use the exact phrase for the title and the opening headline. Of course, the phrase would be sprinkled down the page as well, but the title and headline were strong ranking factors. Today, this won't work (at least for the long-term), so don't use a single keyword phrase as either the title or headline, or both. Titles and headlines should be crafted to draw the reader in. They can include topic-related phrases, but don't stuff, and above all, **write them for humans**.

While we are on the topic of page titles, make sure that no two pages on your site share the same title. This also goes for Meta descriptions if you use them. No two pages should contain the same Meta description, and that includes a "template" description that just substitutes a word or phrase each time it's used (as is typical on doorway pages).

• **Written for the search engine or the visitor?**

We've touched on this several times already, but it is so important that I am including it as a separate bullet point. Was the content written for a human or for the search engines? If the latter, or you are not sure, then that piece of content needs some work.

• **Hidden text on the page?**

One way that webmasters have tried to fool the search engines is with hidden text that contains keyword phrases. Hidden text can be achieved a few different ways, but perhaps the simplest is white text on a white background.

To check for hidden text, open the webpage in a browser and click on it somewhere. Now press CTRL+A (command + A on a Mac computer) to select all. Everything on the page will become selected, including anything that may be hidden. Check to make sure that all of text on the page is visible. Any hidden text that is found should be removed immediately.

• **Visible blocks of text that are only there for the search engines.**

An example of this is when a web page lists "incoming search terms", like this one:

Incoming search terms:

- food presentation ideas
- food presentation
- fruit decoration images
- funny food presentation
- fruit art with kids
- fruits foods pictures
- garnishing with vegetables
- picture of joke flower
- food wallpaper
- funny food garnish

What is the point of that list?

Does it in any way help the visitor?

Lists like this serve one purpose only – to add keywords to the page to try to make it rank better in Google. Therefore, according to Google, it is spam.

Incoming search term lists are not the only type of block you'll find on web pages. On travel sites, I've often seen long lists of towns or cities. They are often not hyperlinked to relevant sections of the site, so only serve to add keywords to a page.

Any block of text on your page that is only there to increase keywords on that page, really do need to be removed ASAP.

• Over-optimization of the page as a whole.

Google has gone out of its way to stop webmasters over-optimizing their sites because SEO is spoiling their otherwise great search results by showing pages that don't deserve to be at the top on merit.

While a lot of over-optimization relates to the backlinks of a website (and we'll cover that later), it also applies to what is on the website itself.

Take a look at the pages on your site and see whether a single phrase is used more than you might expect, thus making it obvious the phrase(s) was an intended target. If you find any, also check to see whether:

• Links to that page are using that phrase as anchor text?

• Is that phrase also in key areas of your web page, like title, meta description, H1 header, opening paragraph, ALT tag, image title tags, bolded, italic etc.

As a general rule, SEO should be "invisible".

I don't mean that there is none. Just that what is there should be discrete and not obvious and in-your-face.

There are WordPress plugins available that are designed to help check your on-page SEO. These are keyword driven checks and I think they are a bad idea. Content should NOT be keyword driven, it should be visitor driven.

If you have been using an SEO plugin that checks for placement of keywords in an article, I'd recommend using it to de-optimize your articles (removing phrases from places they really don't need to be) and once done, delete the plugin.

• **Is your content driven by keywords, or by what the visitors want?**

This is always a good check to make. Ask yourself whether the content you write on your site is driven by keyword research, or driven by what your visitors want.

I'm not saying you cannot use keywords in your content, of course you can. My point is this; instead of thinking you have to write an article about the phrase "tablet vs. laptop":

Keyword	Approximate CPC (Search) ?
☐ tablet v laptop ▾	€4.11

.. just because it commands a high cost per click, consider writing an article on "Advantages and disadvantages of using a tablet instead of a laptop".

OK, it could be the same article right? However, thinking about your content in terms of the visitor instead of your keyword research tool should ensure your content has a fighting chance of pleasing Google. Of course, you could include the phrase "tablet vs. laptop" in your article if you wanted (and it made sense to do so). I'm just suggesting a different approach to choosing the topics you write about.   Think what article the visitor wants to see first, then go and see which keywords are relevant to the article.

• **Does your content reflect search/visitor intent?**

Does your web page offer a good match for the search terms it's found for?

In other words, if you rank #1 in Google for "natural pain killers", but your web page only mention one in passing while discussing an array of pharmaceutical pain killers, is the visitor going to be happy with your page? I doubt it. For starters, they wanted pain killers plural and secondly they wanted natural pain killers and your page is mostly about pharmaceutical pain killers.

As we've seen, Google have ways of measuring how happy visitors are with your page, like bounce rate, time on site, social signals, visitor interaction etc.

Therefore *it's important you don't try to rank for phrases that are a poor match for your content*.

• Does your page provide something not already in the top 10?

Does your content provide something that is not already available in the top 10 of Google? If not, why should it replace one of those pages in the top 10?

So what type of things can you add to your web page to make it stand out from the rest? What can you include that the other top 10 pages don't have?

Things like:

• Personal stories

• Your own opinion

• Your own unique thoughts, ideas etc.

• Images or photographs that work with the topic of your page.

• Visitor interaction – maybe a poll asking for visitor opinion. A poll coupled with an active comments section would create a great resource, especially if the topic of your page was a little controversial.

Content quality checklist

Look at every page on your website. The following checklist should be applied to your content.

• If the page is essentially an article, could it appear in a magazine?

• Is this the type of content that people would want to bookmark?

• Would people like to share this content with their friends and followers?

• Check a sentence or two in Google to see if your content has been used (illegally or otherwise) on other websites. If it has, you need to implement Google authorship immediately and hope Google gives you authorship of your content. Also, contact any webmaster that is illegally displaying your content and ask them to remove it (see the article I linked to in this section of the book on copyright infringement).

• If it's a product review, is it unbiased? Does it tell the good, the bad and the ugly? Does your review add information that gives opinions and views which are not found on the manufacturer's website, or any other website for that matter?

• If you use affiliate links, do your visitors know they are affiliate links? They should!

• Read each piece of content and look for keyword stuffing. Does it read naturally for a human, or was it written for a search engine? If any word or phrase appears more often than might be expected in a naturally written piece of content, then re-write it.

• How much fluff is in your article? Try to make sure your content does not contain fluff and filler. Get rid of any sentences that are only there to increase word count. If you have to remove a lot of fluff, perhaps the article could benefit from a total re-write.

• Do any two (or more) articles overlap in terms of what they talk about? Is the same information mentioned on more than one page of the site? If so, get rid of the duplication.

• Check your sitemap for possible problems. Are there any entries with similar filenames or titles that may indicate the articles cover the same/similar material? Are there any entries that suggest content was written around keywords rather than around the interests of the visitor? If so, get rid (or re-write) all content that was not written specifically for the visitors.

• Check all of your page titles and headlines to make sure that you don't use the same title and headline on any given piece of content. Headlines and titles should work together to entice the visitor. They should be written for the visitor and not for the search engines.

• Make sure you don't use the same title on more than one page.

• Check Meta descriptions if you use them. These should not be keyword stuffed, and again, should be written for the visitor to tell them what the content is about.

• Make sure you don't use the same Meta description (or "templated" description) on more than one page.

• Check each page for hidden text and remove any that you find.

• Are there any visible blocks of text on your pages that are only there for the search engines? If yes, get rid of them.

• SEO should be "invisible". Is it difficult to spot intentional SEO on your pages/site?

• Is your content driven by keywords or by what the visitor wants? Check... If it's the former, you need to clean up the content.

• Check to see what keywords your pages are being found for. Does your page reflect the searchers intent for these keywords?

• Does your page provide something not found on any other web page?

Checklist Point #10 – Inbound link profiles

Getting links back to your website has always been one of the main jobs for any webmaster. Although Google didn't like it, they did tolerate the behavior, at least until they rolled out their Penguin. Overnight, established websites dropped from the rankings. Pages that had been holding the top slot for years suddenly disappeared.

Google had done something that no-one believed they ever would. They started to enforce their guidelines relating to "link schemes".

> *"**Any links intended to manipulate a site's ranking** in Google search results may be **considered part of a link scheme**. This includes any behavior that manipulates links to your site, or outgoing links from your site. Manipulating these links may affect the quality of our search results, and as such **is a violation of Google's Webmaster Guidelines**."*
>
> (http://bit.ly/unP5N2)

Any site that is seen to be participating in link schemes is in danger of ranking loss. However, even worse than that, any site that HAD participated in link schemes is also in danger. That means if you have a site that you are now running "by the book", but you had been involved in some dodgy link schemes in the past, your rankings could be seriously affected.

Google are looking for unnatural links. That is, links that have clearly been built by the webmaster, usually, though not always, on a large scale, and often of low quality.

To put it bluntly, **Google don't want you to build links to your own website**, at least not links whose sole purpose is to improve your rankings. As you look through your own backlink profile, it's important to be able to identify links that may be causing your site a problem and deal with them accordingly. These include any links that Google would consider part of a "link scheme".

Now, before I go through the kinds of links that will hurt your site, let me be clear about one thing. If your site received a penalty because of its backlinks, cleaning up those backlinks WILL NOT return your site to the same "pre-penalty" rankings. The reason is that your pre-penalty rankings were achieved WITH these spammy links, while they were still being counted by Google. These spammy links were helping your pages rank. Removing them means your pages don't have the same inbound links, and therefore won't rank as high. So, while cleaning up your links is vital to your long term success, don't expect that cleaning them up will put your old rankings back. For that, you'll need to build new, stronger, authority links to your site to replace the ones you've deleted/removed.

Ok, it's important to know what constitutes a bad link. Before we look at that though, it's probably better if I tell you how to find the links that point to your site.

Finding backlinks to your website

There are several tools you can use, some free, some paid. However, the one you should all be using as part of your backlink search is Google Webmaster Tools (which is free).

Google Webmaster Tools
(http://bit.ly/11xlJo)

If you don't have an account with Google Webmaster Tools, you should get one. If Google wants to notify you of problems with your site (spiderability, spyware detected, links warnings, etc), they'll do it through Google Webmaster Tools (GWT).

GWT will show you the links that Google know about.

Just go to the **Traffic** section of the sidebar, and then select **Links to your site**:

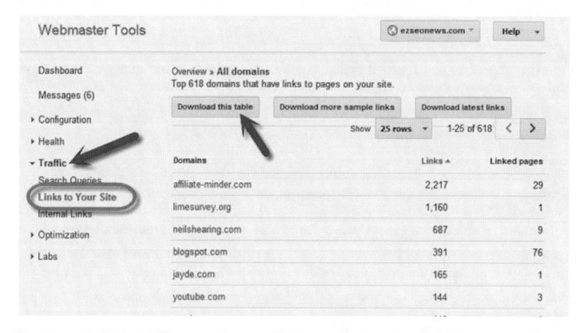

There is a link at the top of the table allowing you to download all of the links in the table. You'll get data on how many times a domain links to your site, and how many pages on your site it links to.

You can inspect the backlinks from any of these domains by clicking the hyperlink in the **Domains** column.

For example, in the list of domains pointing at my site, I didn't recognize a domain called **greenscapemedia.com.** I clicked the hyperlink to see what pages on my site it is linking to:

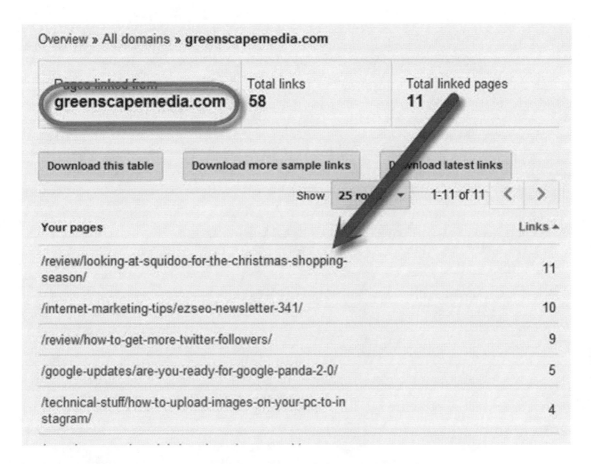

This page tells me that greenscapemedia.com has a total of 58 links to my site.

The table lists my pages that the domain links to, and how many links point to each of these pages.

I can see that greenscapemedia.com links to 11 of my pages in total (the table tells me it's showing 1-11 of 11 pages).

I can also see that this domain has 11 links pointing at the top URL, 10 pointing to the next, 9 to the next and so on (the links column on the right).

I can view the URLs on greenscapemedia.com that link to any of my pages by clicking the URL hyperlink (arrow in the screenshot) for my page. If I check the links pointing to my "Squidoo for Christmas Shopping" post, I can see:

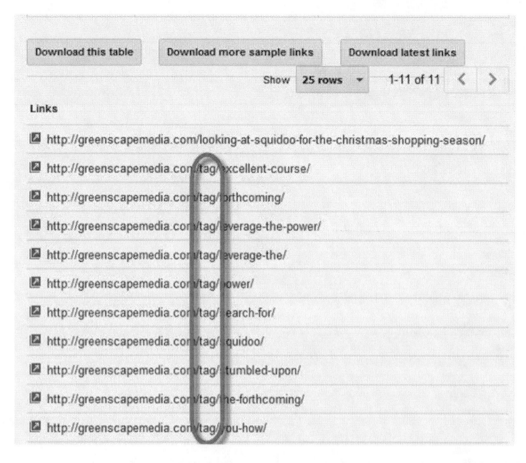

In this case, it looks like one "article" on greenscapemedia.com is linking to my page and the other 10 links are on tag pages. I'd guess that those tag pages are the various tags this webmaster used when tagging his main article. I can also see that this webmaster stole my title (and therefore probably part of my article).

I can click these hyperlinks to open these pages in my web browser. This allows me to view the links to my site.

The URL at the top of this list is basically a spam page and one that I would try to get removed if my site had been penalized for dodgy backlinks.

I should now go back and check the 10 other pages on my site that greenscapemedia.com is linking to.

What I love about GWT is that you get to see the link data that Google has for your website. I'm sure they probably don't show you everything, but it really is a great start to see their backlink data. GWT is always my first stop to find any problematic backlinks.

SEO Spyglass

SEO Spyglass is a commercial tool, though there is a free version to get you started. The free version won't let you save your data and there may be other limitations, but it can find links that aren't reported in GWT.

SEO Spyglass (http://bit.ly/O0kSe)

Essentially, with SEO Spyglass, you type in the URL of your site and the software does the rest. It goes off to numerous sources to find backlinks to your website.

SEO Spyglass gives you masses of information about the links to your site. Things like:

• The URL that links to your site,

• Which page it links to,

• The anchor text,

• Whether the link it dofollow or nofollow,

• IP address,

• Domain age,

• How many links per page

• Lots, lots more.

SEO Spyglass really is a great tool for finding backlinks and link data for your site.

Ahrefs

This site is a popular one, for good reason. It does an excellent job of finding links to your website. The free version is very limited, so to get the best out of this tool, you need a paid subscription.

Ahrefs (http://ahrefs.com/)

Majestic SEO

Majestic SEO has a really useful free option and more comprehensive paid plans.

Majestic SEO (http://www.majesticseo.com/)

To see what is included for free, view this page:

http://bit.ly/gSfcyu

I'd recommend you sign up for a free account. Once you have done that, you can create a free Report for your domain. This involves uploading a text file to your server to prove the domain is yours. Once confirmed, Majestic SEO starts to analyze links to your domain. You'll then find the report in your reports screen. See the post above for a good introduction to using Majestic SEO. It includes an excellent video "webinar".

Ok, so you know now how to find the links, but how do you evaluate them?

Link schemes

Remember this quote from earlier?

> *"Any links intended to manipulate a site's ranking in Google search results may be considered part of a link scheme. This includes any behavior that manipulates links to your site, or outgoing links from your site. Manipulating these links may affect the quality of our search results, and as such is a violation of Google's Webmaster Guidelines."*

Link schemes include "any links intended to manipulate a site's ranking in Google search results".

Here are the schemes that can get you into trouble. You should check your site to make sure you are not engaging in these activities:

• **Buying or selling links that pass PageRank**. If your site has bought links, or sells links, then Google will probably come after you. Please note that when I say "buying", I don't necessarily mean that money changes hands. You could pay for a backlink in any number of ways – goods, services, free products, etc. If a webmaster has taken any kind of "reward" to host your links, then they are considered part of a link scheme. This even includes links found in product reviews, where you have given the webmaster a free copy of your product in exchange for the review and backlink.

• **Partner pages.** These were all the rage 10 years ago. You put up a partner page on your site and linked to other websites in return for a link back. These were also commonly called resource pages. Get rid of any links on a resource/partner page that are reciprocated (i.e., those sites that link back to yours).

• **Linking to undesirable neighborhoods.** If you link to any other site on the web, you are responsible for that link. Google sees links as votes for another website, so if you link to spammy websites, or even websites unrelated to your content, be warned, you could be penalized for it.

One of the places that webmasters unknowingly link to these bad neighborhoods is in the comments section of their website. When people leave comments, they often leave their URL, which could end up as an active link in the comments section on your website. Even if the link looks good now, there is nothing to stop the author of that comment redirecting it later to a porn site, or other undesirable website that you would not want to be associated with. Because of this, I'd recommend you make comment links nofollow. At least this way you are telling Google that you don't necessarily endorse that link.

• **Automated backlinks**. Backlinks built in an automated fashion using software and/or spun content will cause you problems. Not only are the backlinks generated by these tools of low quality, they are also fairly easy for search engines to identify. If you have backlinks built in this way, try your best to remove them.

• **Links in articles that you publish on other websites, where the anchor text is clearly trying to manipulate the rank of your web page.**

Here is an example that Google uses within their guidelines:

> Links that are inserted into articles with little coherence, for example:
> most people sleep at night. you can buy _cheap blankets_ at shops. a blanket
> keeps you warm at night. you can also buy a wholesale heater. It produces
> more warmth and you can just turn it off in summer when you are going on
> _france vacation_.

See how the anchor texts within the body of this article are keyword phrases? These are clearly an attempt to manipulate rankings and Google will get you for it.

If you write articles for other sites (e.g. guest blogs), I'd recommend that you use a resource box at the end of the article, and link to your homepage using either the site name, or site URL as the anchor text. If you want to include a link within the body of the article, I'd suggest using either the URL of the page you are linking to, or its title/headline as the anchor text. These are far more natural than keyword-focused anchor text.

• **Low quality links in general, but Google specifically mentions low-quality directory and bookmark sites.**

I know there are a lot of tempting backlinking gigs on fivver.com, but don't use them. Once you have been submitted to hundreds of low quality directories or bookmark services, you won't be able to get those links taken down, so the damage is permanent.

Other types of low quality links include any type of "profile link" that is clearly only being used for the backlink.

Forum signature links are also bad for your rankings. If you are a member of a forum and you want to include a link to your site in your signature, use your site name or URL as the anchor text. Using a keyword phrase is clearly only trying to get your page to rank better for that keyword phrase.

• **Theme & widget backlinks.** In recent years, another link-building "loophole" was to create a template, or maybe a WordPress widget/plugin, that would be given away for free. Anyone using the theme or plugin would have a link inserted into their homepage (usually in the footer), back to the author's website. Google clamped down on this during 2012 and penalized a lot of websites.

• **Site-wide links**. We've talked about this earlier in the book. Any links that appear on all the pages of your site are called site-wide links. An example would be a blogroll on a WordPress site that usually lists "favorite blogs" in the sidebar. However, site-wide links have been abused by people buying them on other sites, so Google have hit them hard.

I know we all have navigation on our sites, and some items do get placed on every page of the site. However, pay particular attention to any site-wide links that use a keyword phrase as the anchor text. These are the ones that are more likely to get you into trouble. You know the ones – a "make money online" or "buy cheap contact lenses" link in the footer of all pages on your site. All site-wide links with keyword rich anchor text need to be looked at, and changed.

As you can see, link building has just become a lot more difficult. If you listen to Google, they'll just tell you to write great content and the links will come naturally. It's really not that simple because webmasters are not so generous about linking out to other websites. We therefore do need to find ways to get backlinks that at least appear to be more natural. My companion book "SEO 2013 & Beyond" has ideas for these (see appendix at the back for details of my other books).

In terms of critiquing/cleaning up your backlink profile, your job is to try to identify them and clean up ALL poor quality links pointing to your site. The job then is to build new, better quality links to replace them.

Make a list of all bad links to your site

You really do need to make a list of all bad links pointing to your site and then contact each webmaster in turn to ask them to remove the link. Successful or not (and in most cases it won't be), document every attempt you make. When you have the data to show you have tried to clean up your backlinks, you can then approach Google using their **Disavow tool** (http://bit.ly/TtN3aZ).

The disavow tool tells Google that you want these links ignored AND that you have tried to clean them up. There are no guarantees with the disavow tool, but it is worth a go when you consider your final option, which is moving the site to a new domain and beginning the backlink process from scratch.

There is a good article here that describes one person's positive results using the disavow tool:

http://mz.cm/TaGVel

Other specific things to look out for in your backlink profile

1. **Diverse IPs** – Is there a good spread of IP addresses for the pages that link to your website? A lot of links from very similar IP addresses may indicate a blog network, or links from self-owned domains.
2. **Lots of links from the same domain** could indicate site-wide links that may need to be removed. If the site is authority and you get traffic from that site, then you might want to leave those links intact. If they are site-wide on low quality domains, then get them removed.
3. **Too many keyword phrase anchor texts**. Google Penguin is looking at the anchor text of inbound links. If you have a lot of links with the exact same anchor text, then is that natural? If it is the name of your site, then yes. If it is commercial keyword phrases that you want your site to rank for, then no. In 2012, anchor text links became a lot less important. My advice is to water these down significantly and aim for links designed to increase your authority, i.e., using your domain name, brand name or domain URL as the anchor text.
4. **Too many backlinks on low quality directories**. We mentioned this earlier.
5. **Backlinks from spun content**. This is a huge problem if you ever used automated backlink software to create backlinks using spun content. Spun content is one of the deadly sins of SEO and Google are on the warpath. They are getting better and better at detecting it, so if you find backlinks in spun content, do your best to get them taken down. Sometimes this type of backlink is easy to spot by looking at the titles of the pages containing the backlinks. Here is an example of backlinks I found in GWT for one site that clearly used spun content for backlinks:

Links

http://goarticles.com/article/Is-Serrapeptase-The-solution-to-Dupuytren-s-Disease/

http://goarticles.com/article/Serrapeptase-A-Feasible-Therapy-For-Numerous-Sclerosis/

http://goarticles.com/article/Serrapeptase-A-potential-Strategy-to-Multiple-Sclerosis/

http://goarticles.com/article/Utilizing-Serrapeptase-to-alleviate-Bodily-Discomfort/

This type of backlink is VERY bad for your site. Fortunately, these links were on the GoArticles website. I contacted them about the spammy nature of these articles and they took them down.

Inbound link profile checklist

Check the links pointing to your site using the tools mentioned in this book. If you only use one, I'd recommend GWT.

Have you participated in link schemes? This includes:

• Buying or selling links to pass Page Rank? Get rid of paid links.

• Do you have a partner / resources page on your site containing reciprocal links? Remove all links that are reciprocated.

• Are you linking (knowingly or unknowingly perhaps via the comments system) to bad neighborhoods? Get these links removed

• Do you have backlinks created by automated tools? Try to get these taken down.

• Are backlinks coming in from content that was spun? Try to get these taken down.

• Are the backlinks found in the body of articles linking to your site using keyword rich anchor text? If so, I'd recommend you change these keyword links and use your domain name, brand name, domain URL or title/headline of the article, as the link text.

• Are there any low quality directory or bookmarking links? These will cause you trouble so if you cannot remove them, they should be added to your list of links to disavow, if you eventually have to do that.

• Are there any backlinks to your site from themes or widgets that you have created? If so, you need to deactivate those links.

• Are there any links on your website that link out to other websites from themes or widgets you may be using? If so, remove them.

• Are there site-wide links pointing to your site from low quality websites? If so, they need to be removed. Site-wide links from high quality websites are probably OK, and I wouldn't remove those except as a last resort.

• Are your links from a diverse set of IP addresses? If not, get more links on different IP addresses.

• Do you have links from other websites you own? Are those links purely to help your pages rank better or is there a good reason to cross-link. If there is no good reason to cross-link the sites, remove those links.

• Are there lots of links from the same domain? If the domain is low quality, get them removed.

• Is there a high percentage of inbound links using keywords phrases you are targeting as anchor text? If so, I'd advise you to water these down. Include more links that use the domain/brand name, URL or title/headline of the content you are linking to.

Real-world examples of bad SEO

Modern SEO is not just about keeping the search engines happy, it's first and foremost about keeping your visitors happy. Their time on the site, including bounce rate and social interaction with your pages, are increasingly important signals that the search engines use to help decide how good your content is.

In this section, I want to highlight some examples of bad SEO that I found while critiquing a number of websites.

An example of bad navigation

This was the sidebar on the website:

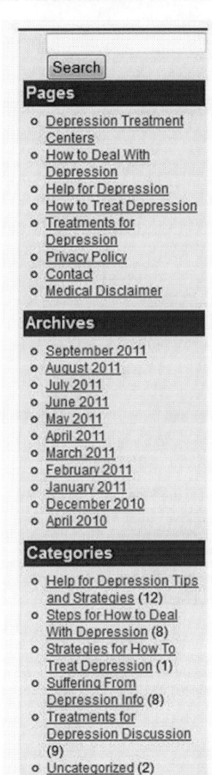

There are 4 sections to this navigation bar and I should also mention that this was a WordPress site.

The first is the search box, which is a good thing, though this was the default WordPress search box which isn't much use.

Under that is a section labeled "**Pages**". Pages in WordPress are one of two forms of content, the other being "Posts". This site seems to be mixing pages and posts in a way that makes me think the webmaster had no clear plan for the structure of the site. Either that, or the site was built initially with pages, but the webmaster wanted to add more content at a later date and so decided upon posts.

My own advice is to restrict the use of Pages in WordPress to the "legal pages" and use posts for all content written for the visitor. There are of course some exceptions, but this is a good general rule that allows you to make use of the excellent structural organization built into WordPress itself.

The next area of the navigation bar is an "**Archives**" section.

What is the purpose of this?

Does it help the visitor?

If this site was news based, where someone might like to check a news story from last month, then the archives section would be worth considering. However, this site isn't. In fact it's a fairly static site with little or no new content being added. Therefore the archive section just clutters an already cluttered navigation system.

The final area of the navigation menu is the "**Categories**" section. This is actually a useful section for visitors because they'll be able to find relevant

POSTS. Note I put "posts" in capital letters, because PAGES won't be included in the category system (which only shows posts). Therefore the PAGES listed in the top section of the navigation menu won't be found using this category menu at the bottom.

You can see how the navigation system on this site is not very well organized and would only serve to confuse a visitor.

Things actually get worse. This website has a sitemap, which you can see here:

URL	Priority	Change Frequency	LastChange (GMT)
http:// /	100%	Daily	2011-11-18 23:36
http:// /medical-disclaimer/	30%	Weekly	2011-11-18 23:36
http:// /contact/	30%	Weekly	2011-11-18 23:36
http:// /how-to-treat-depression/	30%	Weekly	2011-11-10 23:57
http:// /help-for-depression/	30%	Weekly	2011-07-01 23:44
http:// /how-to-deal-with-depression/	30%	Weekly	2010-12-18 17:49
http:// /depression-treatment-centers/	30%	Weekly	2010-12-18 17:45
http:// /treatments-for-depression/	30%	Weekly	2010-12-18 17:32
http:// /privacy-policy/	30%	Weekly	2010-12-15 20:50

Generated with Google Sitemap Generator Plugin for WordPress by Arne Brachhold. This XSLT template is released under GPL.

The sitemap only has 9 entries, and that included the homepage and three "legal pages". Only 5 content pages were included, yet we can see from the sidebar navigation that this site did have 40+ posts and a few content pages.

A sitemap should list all important URLs on the site, most notably the posts. Disclaimers and other "legal" pages can be left off the sitemap. The main role of the sitemap is to make sure the search engines can find the important pages on your site.

Overall then, the navigation system on this site (which I believe has now been taken down since I originally critiqued it for the owner), is a good example of what not to do.

If you would like to test out your SEO sleuthing skills, have a look at the pages in the sidebar menu (Pages section) and see another major mistake that this site made. Hint: Look at the page titles.

An example of over-optimization

Have a look at this web page:

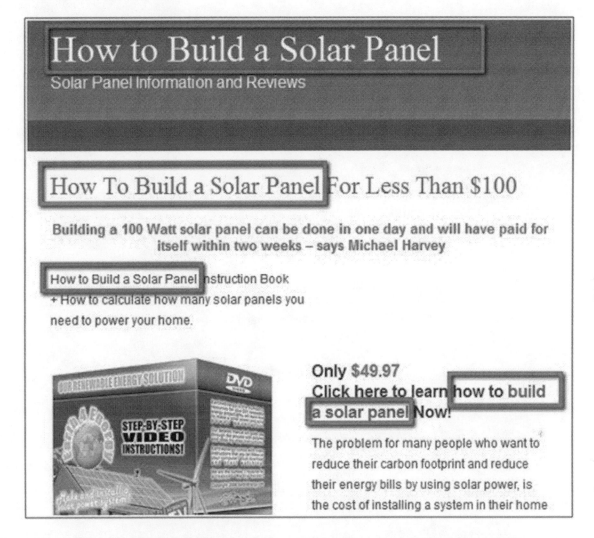

The webmaster was clearly trying to rank this page for "How to build a solar panel".

The Header section of this page used the text "How to build a solar panel" in an H1 header. Then there is an opening H1 header that has the same phrase (that's two H1 headers on the same page which is never good). The exact same phrase then appears twice more and this is all ABOVE THE FOLD. This phrase is also in the title tag of the page, plus the Meta description of the page. It is also found in the ALT text of an image on the page.

This is an extreme example of over-optimization.

Example of fake comments

Here are the comments on a website I was critiquing:

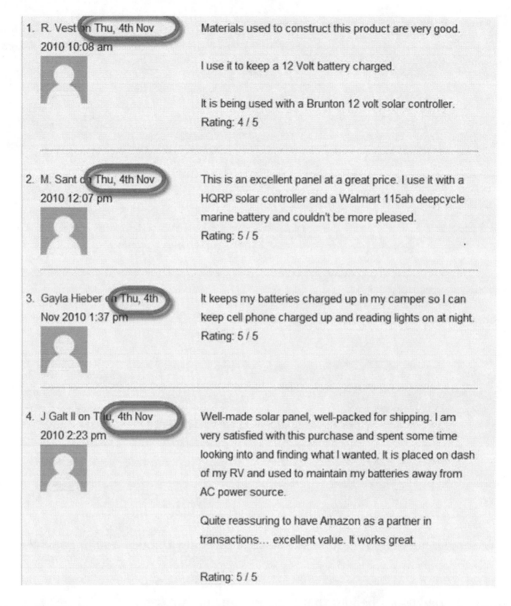

1. R. Vest on Thu, 4th Nov 2010 10:08 am

    Materials used to construct this product are very good.

    I use it to keep a 12 Volt battery charged.

    It is being used with a Brunton 12 volt solar controller.
    Rating: 4 / 5

2. M. Sant on Thu, 4th Nov 2010 12:07 pm

    This is an excellent panel at a great price. I use it with a HQRP solar controller and a Walmart 115ah deepcycle marine battery and couldn't be more pleased.
    Rating: 5 / 5

3. Gayla Hieber on Thu, 4th Nov 2010 1:37 pm

    It keeps my batteries charged up in my camper so I can keep cell phone charged up and reading lights on at night.
    Rating: 5 / 5

4. J Galt II on Thu, 4th Nov 2010 2:23 pm

    Well-made solar panel, well-packed for shipping. I am very satisfied with this purchase and spent some time looking into and finding what I wanted. It is placed on dash of my RV and used to maintain my batteries away from AC power source.

    Quite reassuring to have Amazon as a partner in transactions… excellent value. It works great.

    Rating: 5 / 5

Notice that all of the comments were on the same day within 4 hours of each other? That in itself is not unheard of, but the comments themselves made me suspicious because they each included a rating out of 5 (and none of them had Gravatar images).

To check the comments, I took a sentence from one of them and searched Google for that sentence (in quotes):

> "It keeps my batteries charged up in my camper so I can keep cell phone cl

| Web | Images | Maps | Shopping | More ▾ | Search tools |

15 results (0.36 seconds)

Ad related to "It keeps my batteries charged up in my camper so I ... ⓘ

Ask an RV Tech Online - Technicians Will Answer in Minutes
rv.justanswer.com/Camper-RV
Questions Answered Every 9 Seconds.
Lawyer - Doctor - Nurse - Veterinarian

Amazon.com: Customer Reviews: HQRP 20W Mono-crystalline ...
www.amazon.com/HQRP-Mono-crystalline.../B002HT09TO
**It keeps my batteries charged up in my camper so I can keep cell phone
charged up and reading lights on at night.** Help other customers find the most
helpful ...

Amazon.com: HQRP 20W Mono-crystalline Solar Panel 20 Watt 12 ...
www.amazon.com › ... › Solar & Wind Power › Solar Panels
**It keeps my batteries charged up in my camper so I can keep cell phone
charged up and reading lights on at night.** Published on March 19, 2010 by Gayla ...

Amazon.com: Gayla Hieber's review of HQRP 20W Mono-crystalline ...
www.amazon.com/review/RW67BDW88G8WU
**It keeps my batteries charged up in my camper so I can keep cell phone
charged up and reading lights on at night.** Gayla Hieber March 19, 2010. Overall:
5.0 out ...

Looking for customer reviews for HQRP 20W Mono-crystalline Solar ...
askville.amazon.com › ... › Shopping › Lawn Garden
2 answers - 8 Jun 2011
**It keeps my batteries charged up in my camper so I can keep cell phone
charged up and reading lights on at night.** 4 of 4 found the following ...

Google found that exact same sentence /comment on 15 web pages, including Amazon.

Could the webmaster have found these comments on Amazon and added them to his website?
Or maybe he paid someone to add comments and they copied them from Amazon?

Whatever the answer, this is bad.

I checked the other "fake" comments on the webpage and every one of them was found on
numerous other websites including Amazon.

Example of sneaky affiliate links

There is nothing wrong with having affiliate links on your website. However, visitors should know that they are affiliate links, and "hidden" affiliate links designed to set a cookie are not a good idea.

One site I critiqued a while ago used the whole of the background of his site (i.e. all the space to the left and right of the main content) as one big affiliate link. Click on the background ANYWHERE and you were directed via an affiliate link to the merchant site. This clearly is not a good idea. As I was critiquing the site I cannot remember how many times I ended up on the merchant site. I can only guess at how annoyed visitors got with this. That was an extreme case.

Here is another case of hidden affiliate links:

Divine Baby Shower Cakes

The centerpiece of any party is a ... of whether to make o how much, can be difficult. Don't options available, you'll have a d

Beautiful Baby Shower Decor

Decorations are a vital part of an ... important because the set the tone for a party from the choosing a color set that works

Baby Shower Theme Ideas

It can be hard to decide on a the pamper the new mom with a trip diapers, onesies, and baby acce some of ... below may ma

On this page, the webmaster had hyperlinked all of the images to Amazon with an affiliate link. The landing page was an Amazon search results page for the phrase **baby shower invitations**.

Why do this?

Does it in some way help the visitor?

Or is it an attempt to set a cookie on Amazon?

Of course, it could have been a genuine mistake, but this type of thing is not adding to the visitor experience.

An example of how NOT to create a contact us page

On the contact page of one affiliate site I critiqued, I found this:

Contact Information

If you have any questions about satellite TV systems or service, please call DISH Network or DIRECTV's toll-free telephone number, or click on the link listed below.

DISH Network

For questions about DISH Network satellite tv systems or service, contact U.S. Dish:

By phone: 1-888-228-0942

Online: Click here for U.S. Dish online support

DIRECTV

For questions about DIRECTV satellite TV systems or service, contact U.S. Direct:

By phone: 1-866-529-6828

Online: Click here for U.S. Direct online support

Instead of contact details for the site, it provided contact details of two merchants instead. That means visitors have no way to contact the webmaster of this website.

It also makes it look like this webmaster is pretending to be the merchant (or a website owned by the merchant).

Your contact page should give your visitors YOUR contact details so they can contact YOU! This not only builds trust, but is also a basic requirement of doing business online.

Incidentally, the same website also had a link in their menu labeled "Affiliate Information". This is typically only something found on a merchant site. On the Affiliate Information page, this website linked to the affiliate programs of the two merchants!

Example of a bad inbound link profile

Deciding what is a good or bad inbound link profile is quite a challenge, I mean what does a natural profile look like. How about this one:

Webpage PageRank	▾ %
PR: —	96.3% (1134)
PR: 1	1.6% (19)
PR: 0	0.8% (10)
PR: 3	0.8% (10)
PR: 2	0.3% (4)
PR: 4	0.0% (0)
PR: 5	n nox /n\

There are links fromPR1, PR2 and PR3 pages, which is good. However, these amount to just 2.7% of all inbound links. A whopping 96.3% of inbound links (that's 1134 links) came from web pages where the Page Rank was N/A (the lowest possible rank, often found on very new pages, pages that have been penalized or pages of very poor quality).

This profile indicates to me that the webmaster went for quantity, not quality, and from some very poor sources. I'd expect to see this type of profile on a site that used automated backlinking software. This is exactly the type of thing that Google Penguin will bite you for.

148

Example of bad internal linking

Internal linking of pages on a website is done to help the visitor. Done correctly, it can help guide visitors to more information about certain topics.

On one website I critiqued, something strange was going on with the internal linking. Here are two examples of the type of internal linking I found:

ccount while others w only apply
es actual dollars for the **consumer**.

Finding the best credit card de for your spe
credit cards can often be a plicated, confu
have little or **no experience** managing cards.

The anchor text in the first example was "consumer", and the anchor text in the second example was "no experience".

When you internally link pages on your site using contextual links, the anchor texts MUST be related to the page you are linking to. The anchor text must also be fairly self-serving, not leaving anything to the imagination as to what the destination is about. I mean, what would a visitor think the destination URL is about if the link text is "consumer"? What about "no experience"?

The "consumer" link went to an article on "mileage credit cards".

The "no experience" link went to a page on "credit card debt relief".

Do these help the visitor? Nope! The only point I can think of is that the webmaster was trying to make sure their pages were crawled and indexed (and Page Rank passed around), so added more links to them in this way.

Here is another one:

eveal a **secret weapon** that you can use aga
cuss this strategy, let us just look briefly at th
d companies to recruit you as their customer.

What has "secret weapon" got to do with any article on credit cards?

Do you see the problem with these?

One final example on this site is this internal link:

6. Borrow against your 401k

When you **take a loan against your 401k** you are paying
your goal is a one time payoff of credit card debt it can
than to throw away 29% interest to a credit lending insti

The anchor text "take a loan against your 401k" linked to a page that did not include the word 401K!

Where to go from here

"Make sure that your site adds value. Provide unique and relevant content that gives users a reason to visit your site first".

In 2012, SEO changed forever. Google became far less tolerant of activities that they see as rank manipulation. Google want to serve web pages that offer their visitors the best possible experience, and that means your primary focus should be on your Visitor. Not Google, not a keyword research tool, and certainly not automated tools that claim to do your SEO for you.

As webmasters, we have been given a choice. Stick to Google's rules, or lose out on free traffic from the world's biggest search engine.

Sure, there will always be someone advertising the next greatest "loophole" to beat the system, and they'll even have examples to prove their loophole works. These examples may even go against everything that Google wants and break all the rules, which will make them tempting to some. However, these loopholes are short-lived. My advice to you is to ignore anyone that tries to sell you a loophole, a trick, or anything else that is "under Google's radar". If you want long-lasting results, stick to the rules - Google's rules.

The SEO in this book (and in my SEO 2013 & Beyond Kindle book) is the SEO I use on a daily basis. It's the SEO I teach my students, and it's the SEO that I know works. For those that embrace the recent changes, SEO has actually become easier as we no longer have to battle against other sites whose SEO was done 24/7 by an automated tool or army of cheap labor. Those sites have largely been removed, and that levels the playing field nicely.

I assume you bought this book to help you clean up a site of your own. Just go through the checklist included at the end of this book, working your way through the points.

Oh, and good luck!

Appendix - The checklist

Checkpoint 1 - The domain name
• Exact Match Domain (EMD)? If yes, then be aware that this will work against you and you'll need to de-optimize the site for the phrase in the domain name.

• Keyword stuffed? There isn't much you can do with this other than move the site to a better domain. Keyword stuffed domains look spammy and don't instill much confidence in visitors. Unless there is good reason to keep the domain (like it still makes good income or ranks well), I'd consider moving the site to a better, brandable domain.

• Has your domain never ranked properly? If not, then check its history at the Way Back Machine. Consider a reconsideration request at Google if it looks like the domain was used before.

Checkpoint 2 - Web page real estate
• Resize your browser to 1024x768 and see what loads above the fold. Is there useful content? Are there too many adverts? If there are too many ads, especially above the fold, consider removing (or moving) them.

• If you removed all of the adverts from the pages on your site, would those pages still offer the visitor what they are looking for?   If not, then the content is not good enough.

• Does your site have sneaky links in the footer, especially keyword rich anchor text links to your own site or an external site? If so, get rid of them.

Checkpoint 3 - site structure
• Is your navigation intuitive?

• Are all of the pages on your site just one or two clicks away from the homepage?

• Do you have site-wide links in the sidebar?

• Do you have site-wide links in the header?

• Do you have site-wide links in the footer?

NOTE: Site-wide links with keyword-rich anchor text are the most potentially damaging.

• If you have a large site, do you use dynamic menus, which change depending on the section of the site the visitor is viewing?

• Do you have a search box? If it is a WordPress default search box, I highly recommend you switch to a more efficient script, e.g. Google's custom search.

• Do you internally link the pages of your website from within the body of your content, not just via the navigation menus or a related posts menu?

• Is your content organized logically into "silos" where all related content is in the same category or folder? If necessary (e.g. on a large site), do you use sub-folders to help make the navigation more intuitive?

• If you are using WordPress, do you have tags that are only used once or twice? If so, remove them.

• If you are using WordPress, do you have tags that are identical to some of your categories? Never use a phrase for a tag if it is being used (or will be used) as a category.

Checkpoint 4 – Comments

• Does your website have a comments section where visitors can leave their own thoughts and questions?

• Does your website have a Contact Us form?

• If you have comments enabled, are you manually approving all comments? You should be.

• Check through all of the comments on your site and remove any fake or spam comments. In fact, remove any comment whose sole purpose is to get a backlink to a website.

• Make comment links nofollow.

• Going forward, only approve legitimate comments where it is clear the visitor read your content and added to the conversation with their insight.

Checkpoint 5 - Social presence

• Does the website have a presence on Facebook?

• Does the website have a presence on Twitter?

• Does the website have a presence on Google plus?

• Does your website have social sharing buttons that allow your visitors to share your content with their social media followers? You should include Twitter, Facebook and Google plus as a bare minimum.

• Setup Google Authorship for your site and connect your content to your Google plus profile.

Checkpoint 6 - Would you trust this site?

• Does the site have a photo of the webmaster/author of the content?

• Does your site have an About Us page?

• Are Comments enabled?

• Does your site pretend to be a merchant?

• Is the author of your site a recognized authority in the niche/industry?

• Are you using a Gravatar set up on the email address you use for your site?

• Is your business address displayed on the site, preferably with a phone number?

• When was the last time your site was updated?

• If appropriate, are there testimonials, and are they up to date?

• Is the copyright notice on your website the correct year?

• Do you display any trust symbols (if appropriate)

• Check all content for spellings and grammatical errors. Check your navigation systems for these errors as well.

• Are there unanswered comments on your site?

Checkpoint 7 - Bounce rates & time on site
I recommend you install the updated code here (which will give you a more accurate measurement of these parameters):

http://bit.ly/KbUvs9

Once installed and allowed to run for a few weeks, check your bounce rate and time on site at Google Analytics.

• Are your average bounce rates high?

• Are visitors spending a long or short time on your site?

• Look for specific pages where bounce rate is high AND time on site is low. Try to work out why these pages are suffering and fix them.

Checkpoint 8 - Legal pages
Not all of these pages are necessary for all types of website, so check which pages your site needs and add them if they are missing.

• Do you have a privacy page?

- Do you have a disclaimer page?

- Do you have a terms page?

- Do you have a contact page?

- Do you have an about us page?

- Do you have a medical disclaimer page?

- Do you have an email policy page?

- Do you have an outbound link policy page?

Checkpoint 9 - Content quality
Look at every page on your website. The following checklist should be applied to your content.

- If the page is essentially an article, could it appear in a magazine?

- Is this the type of content that people would want to bookmark?

- Would people like to share this content with their friends and followers?

- Check a sentence or two in Google to see if your content has been used (illegally or otherwise) on other websites. If it has, you need to implement Google authorship immediately and hope that Google gives you authorship of your own content. Also, contact any webmaster that is illegally displaying your content and ask them to remove it (see the article I linked to in this section of the book on copyright infringement).

- If it's a product review, is it unbiased? Does it tell the good, the bad and the ugly? Does your review add information, opinion and views that are not found on the manufacturer's website, or any other website for that matter?

- If you use affiliate links, do your visitors know they are affiliate links? They should!

- Read each piece of content and look for keyword stuffing. Does it read naturally for a human, or was it written for a search engine? If any word or phrase appears more often that might be expected in a naturally written piece of content, then re-write it.

- How much fluff is in your article? Try to make sure your content does not contain fluff and filler. Get rid of any sentences that are only there to increase word count. If you have to remove a lot of fluff, perhaps the article could benefit from a total re-write.

- Do any two (or more) articles overlap in terms of what they talk about? Is the same information mentioned on more than one page of the site? If so, get rid of the duplication.

• Check your sitemap for possible problems. Are there any entries with similar filenames or titles that may indicate the articles cover the same/similar material? Are there any entries that suggest content was written around keywords rather than around the interests of the visitor? If so, get rid (or re-write) all content that was not written specifically for the visitors.

• Check all of your page titles and headlines to make sure that you don't use the same title and headline on any given piece of content. Headlines and titles should work together to entice the visitor. They should be written for the visitor and not for the search engines.

• Make sure you don't use the same title on more than one page.

• Check Meta descriptions if you use them. These should not be keyword stuffed, and again, should be written for the visitor to tell them what the content is about.

• Make sure you don't use the same Meta description (or "templated" description) on more than one page.

• Check each page for hidden text and remove any that you find.

• Are there any visible blocks of text on your pages that are only there for the search engines? If so, get rid of them.

• SEO should be "invisible". Can you spot obvious attempts at SEO on your pages/site?

• Is your content driven by keywords or by what the visitor wants? Check... If it's the former, you need to clean up the content.

• Check to see what keywords your pages are being found for. Does your page reflect the searchers intent for these keywords?

• Does your page provide something not found on any other web page?

Checkpoint 10 - Inbound link profiles

Check the links pointing to your site using the tools mentioned in this book. If you only use one, I'd recommend Google Webmaster Tools (GWT).

Have you participated in link schemes? This includes:

• Buying or selling links to pass Page Rank? Get rid of paid links.

• Do you have a partner / resources page on your site containing reciprocal links? Remove all links that are reciprocated.

• Are you linking (knowingly or unknowingly perhaps via the comments system) to bad neighborhoods? Get these links removed

• Do you have backlinks created by automated tools? Try to get these taken down.

• Are backlinks coming in from content that was spun? Try to get these taken down.

• Are the backlinks found in the body of articles linking to your site using keyword rich anchor text? If so, I'd recommend you change these keyword links and use your domain name, brand name, domain URL or title/headline of the article as the link text.

• Are there any low quality directory or bookmarking links? These will cause you trouble and if you cannot remove them, they should be added to your list of links to disavow, if you eventually have to do that.

• Are there any backlinks to your site from themes or widgets that you have created? If so, you need to deactivate those links.

• Are there any links on your website that link out to other websites from themes or widgets you may be using? If so, remove them.

• Are there site-wide links pointing to your site from low quality websites? If so, they need to be removed. Site-wide links from high quality websites are probably OK, and I wouldn't remove those except as a last resort.

• Are your links from a diverse set of IP addresses? If not, get more links on different IP addresses.

• Do you have links from other websites you own? Are those links purely to help your pages rank better or is there a good reason to cross-link. If there is no good reason to cross-link the sites, remove those links.

• Are there lots of links from the same domain? If the domain is low quality, get them removed.

• Is there a high percentage of inbound links using keywords phrases you are targeting as anchor text? If so, I'd advise you to water these down. Include more links that use the domain/brand name, URL or title/headline of the content you are linking to.

Please leave a review on Amazon

If you enjoyed this book, PLEASE leave a review on the Amazon website. You can find the book listing here:

Search Amazon for **B00C25NFSK**

All the best

Andy Williams

More information from Dr. Andy Williams

If you would like more information, tips, tutorials or advice, there are two resources you might like to consider.

The first is my free weekly newsletter over at **ezSEONews.com** offering tips, tutorials and advice to online marketers and webmasters. Just sign up and my newsletter, plus SEO articles, will be delivered to your inbox. I cannot always promise a weekly schedule, but I do try ;)

I also run a course over at **CreatingFatContent.com**, where I build real websites in front of members in "real-time" using my system of SEO.

My Other Kindle Books

Kindle Publishing – Format, Publish & Promote your Books on Kindle

Why Publish on Amazon Kindle?

Kindle publishing has captured the imagination of aspiring writers. Now, more than at any other time in our history, an opportunity is knocking. Getting your books published no longer means sending out hundreds of letters to publishers and agents. It no longer means getting hundreds of rejection letters back. Today, you can write and publish your own books on Amazon Kindle without an agent or publisher.

Is it really possible to make a good income as an Indie author?

The fact that you are reading this book description tells me you are interested in publishing your own material on Kindle. You may have been lured here by promises of quick riches. Well, I have good news and bad. The bad news is that publishing and profiting from Kindle takes work and dedication. Don't just expect to throw up sub-par material and make a killing in sales. You need to produce good stuff to be successful at this. The good news is that you can make a very decent living from writing and publishing for Kindle.

My own success with Kindle publishing

As I explain at the beginning of this book, I published my first Kindle book in August 2012, yet by December 2012, just 5 months later, I was making what many people consider to be a full time income. As part of my own learning experience, I setup a Facebook page in July 2012 to share my Kindle publishing journey (there is a link to the Facebook page inside this book). On that Facebook page, I shared the details of what I did, problems I needed to overcome, I shared my growing income reports, and most of all, I offered help to those who asked for it. What I found was a huge and growing audience for this type of education, and ultimately, that's why I wrote this book.

What's in this book?

This book covers what I have learned on my journey and what has worked for me. I have included sections to answer the questions I myself asked, as well as those questions people asked me. This book is a complete reference manual for successfully formatting, publishing & promoting your books on Amazon Kindle. There is even a section for non-US publishers because there is stuff you specifically need to know.

I see enormous potential in Kindle Publishing and in 2013, I intend to grow this side of my own business. Kindle publishing has been liberating for me and I am sure it will be for you too.

Search Amazon for **B00BEIX34C**

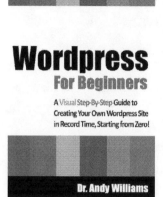

Do you want to build a website but scared it's too difficult?

Building a website was once the domain of computer geeks. Not anymore. WordPress makes it possible for anyone to create and run a professional looking website

While WordPress is an amazing tool, the truth is it does have a steep learning curve, even if you have built websites before. Therefore, the goal of this book is to take anyone, even a complete beginner, and get them building a professional looking website. I'll hold your hand, step-by-step, all the way.

As I was planning this book, I made one decision early on. I wanted to use screenshots of everything, so the reader wasn't left looking for something on their screen that I was describing in text. This book has screenshots. I haven't counted them all, but it must be close to 300. These screenshots will help you find the things I am talking about. They'll help you check your settings and options against a screenshot of mine. You look, compare, and move on to the next section.

With so many screenshots, you may be worried that the text might be a little on the skimpy side. No need to worry there. I have described every step of your journey in great detail. In all, this book has over 35,000 words.

This book will surely cut your learning curve associated with WordPress

Every chapter of the book ends with a "Tasks to Complete" section. By completing these tasks, you'll not only become proficient at using WordPress, you'll become confident & enjoy using WordPress too.

Search Amazon for **B009ZVO3H6**

CSS For Beginners

 Learn CSS with detailed instructions, step-by-step screenshots and video tutorials showing CSS in action on real sites.

Most websites you visit use Cascading Style Sheets (CSS) for everything, from font selection & formatting to layout & design. Whether you are building WordPress sites or traditional HTML websites, this book aims to take the complete beginner to a level where they are comfortable digging into the CSS code and making changes to their own projects. CSS for Beginners will show you how to make all these formatting & layout changes in easy to understand steps.

The book covers the following topics:

- Why CSS is important
- Classes, Pseudo Classes, Pseudo Elements & IDs
- The Float Property
- Units of Length
- Using DIVs
- Tableless Layouts, including how to create 2-column and 3-column layouts
- The Box Model
- Creating Menus with CSS
- Images & Background Images

The hands on approach of this book will get YOU building your own Style Sheets. Also included in this book:

- Over 160 screenshots and 20,000 words detailing every step you need to take
- Full source code for all examples shown
- Video Tutorials

The video tutorials accompanying this book show you:

- How to investigate the HTML & CSS behind any website.
- How to experiment with your own design in real time, and only make the changes permanent on your site when you are ready to implement them.

Note: A basic knowledge of HTML is recommended, although all source code from the book can be downloaded and used as you work through the book

Search Amazon for **B00AFV44NS**

Made in the USA
Lexington, KY
14 February 2014